THE OTHER ROYAL AIR FORCE

First published in 2010 by

Woodfield Publishing Ltd
Bognor Regis ~ West Sussex ~ England ~ PO21 5EL
www.woodfieldpublishing.co.uk

ISBN 1-84683-101-6

The Other Royal Air Force

An RAF Airman's Experiences
Home & Abroad in the 1950s

RAY CLINTON

Woodfield

Woodfield Publishing Ltd

Bognor Regis ~ West Sussex ~ England ~ PO21 5EL
tel 01243 821234 ~ e/m info@woodfieldpublishing.co.uk

Interesting and informative books on a variety of subjects

For full details of all our published titles, visit our website at
www.woodfieldpublishing.co.uk

For my wife Greta
who has 'heard it all before'!

~ CONTENTS ~

About the Author

Ray Clinton lives with his wife Greta in the sleepy market town of Tring in Hertfordshire.

Following four years in the Royal Air Force, supposedly learning how to be an electrician, he worked for the next thirty as a clerk for the largest manufacturing stationers in the country. After being made redundant he spent ten years in Production Control for a computer manufacturer. He is now retired, enabling him to enjoy his family, which includes two delightful teenage grand-daughters.

His hobbies include photography and collecting old 78rpm gramophone records, but his absorbing pastime for over sixty years, continuing still, has been his membership of a local Amateur Operatic and Dramatic Society, appearing in countless plays and musicals. For many years he was involved in its administration, in various offices including General Secretary and Chairman. He has in the past written articles for the Society's magazine and had printed a short account of its history, but this is his first published work.

Introduction

There are many books about the Royal Air Force. Some record the history and development of this illustrious body as it evolved to take its place alongside the other two more senior armed forces, incorporating details of increasingly sophisticated flying machines. Others concentrate on the exploits and dangers of the brave airmen in battle with accounts of their derring-do, lucky mascots and stiff upper-lip demeanour. In all of these the flying personnel and commissioned ranks feature prominently.

For vast numbers of young men, in the years following the Second World War, the Royal Air Force was something else. Conscripts, not volunteers, these National Service "erks" in the lower ranks were removed compulsorily from their homes and occupations, in peacetime, to spend two or more years in unfamiliar corners of Britain and the world. Very few of them ever got to do anything involving aeroplanes and all most of them wanted was to escape from the boredom, the indignity of communal life and the frustration of incomprehensible authority, and return to a normal existence and their loved ones.

They weren't "The Few", they were "The Many" and I, for my sins, was one of them.

Ray Clinton
Tring, Herts, 2010

P.S. This account contains some forthright language which I hope will cause no offence to any of my readers; it would not have been a realistic portrayal without it.

1.   Signing Up

"You're fired!"

"No I'm not!"

We stared at each other in surprise; he because a mature manager did not expect to be answered back by a teenage employee and I because of my courage. But then, I was fairly sure of my rights.

After leaving school at the age of sixteen I had taken a junior position with an electrical company in Watford, some eight miles from home in Hemel Hempstead. I had tried unsuccessfully to get a proper apprenticeship with such a firm but in the 1950s the advent of a spell of National Service at age eighteen created a difficulty. In the internationally unsettled post-war years National Service was compulsory for all medically fit young men, to provide a trained force for the security of the nation. Indentured apprentices could have their period in the armed forces deferred until their professional training was completed and consequently trade apprenticeships were hard to come by, many such places going to the favoured sons and relatives of senior officials in the respective businesses.

Employers were not well pleased to lose staff for a couple of years with the problem on their return of having filled the vacancy, so the unscrupulous would sometimes invent an excuse to terminate a youngster's employment as his eighteenth birthday approached. A law to ban this practice had been passed, as I understood it. So did my manager, it transpired, but we agreed to part company, my final shot being, "Legally, you will be obliged to take me back if I wish you to."

My "call-up papers" were imminent and almost immediately I was summoned to present myself to the local office of the Ministry of Labour and National Service in St Albans on June 26th 1951. There was no difficulty in being accepted into my preferred choice of the Royal Air Force rather than the Army or Navy. It was naturally assumed by all my contemporaries from either Grammar or Secondary Modern schools that service would be in the lower ranks; no mention of a commission was ever made.

At St Albans a friendly sergeant was in charge of proceedings. We sat and contemplated him at his desk and each other. We were a fairly uniform bunch of young men, all of an age and all wearing our best casual clothes except one who was dressed in muddy corduroy trousers and dirty shirt. He had a coarse ruddy complexion and a pronounced limp.

"I works on a farm", he announced, presumably by way of explanation for his appearance.

"Excuse me, sergeant", ventured one of the others, "may I use the lavatory?"

"No lad, save it. You'll be needing it soon."

And indeed he did, when a medical examination eventually got under way, with the requirement of a "sample" from each of us. In turn we had to go behind a screen and undergo a somewhat cursory inspection of our hearts, lungs and more intimate organs. The screens did not provide comprehensive privacy and it was possible partially to see the farmer's boy drop his trousers.

"What happened to your leg?" asked the MO. I could see that it was distorted in several places. More than anything it resembled a crankshaft!

"Oh that! I fell under a tractor."

"But who set it for you?"

"Who what?"

"Which hospital did you go to?"

"I didn't go to no hospital. We ain't got no truck with them."

"But what did you do about it then?"

"I stayed in bed until it felt good enough to walk on."

And that, I gathered, was the end of his military career. The rest of us had no problem being accepted.

An eyesight test came next, by means of the traditional wall-chart, followed by a flip through a book of pretty patterns. I didn't know what that was all about but of course it was the standard test for colour-blindness. I was then asked to sit at a desk, behind which was installed a distinguished elderly gentleman, apparently engrossed in the papers before him.

"What's your name?" he whispered, not looking up at me.

"Raymond Clinton," I whispered back.

"I do the whispering," he whispered. "This is a hearing test."

We were weighed and in rapid succession we passed under a height gauge. The cross-bar was brought down smartly on our heads, causing the knees to buckle in reflex action, so we all went through our service careers with a recorded height less than our actual measurement.

"Now then, how many of you are going to sign on for the extra year?" asked the sergeant.

We stared at him.

"Why should we?" one of us queried.

"Because by serving for three years instead of just the compulsory two you can be taught a proper trade and practise it, which will stand you in good stead when you are back in Civvy Street and looking for a job."

"What would we do then, otherwise, as two-year National Servicemen?"

"Anything that's asked of you, General Duties mostly." He waved the carrot that many of us swallowed. "And there are considerable advantages. As a "regular" you would receive double the wages and double the leave; thirty days a year instead of the thirty days total for a two-year engagement."

I thought all this over.

"Could I be trained properly as an electrician?"

"Yes, lad, certainly. Either as an 'Electrical Mechanic Air', which involves all the electrics on aircraft, or an 'Electrical Mechanic Ground', which is more like your average civilian 'sparks'. There are plenty of other career opportunities," he added for the benefit of the rest of us, "such as 'Air Frame Mechanic', 'Instrument Mechanic', 'Sheet Metal Worker', 'Carpenter' and a host of others, plus various clerical positions."

My late employer had shown no interest in having me taught anything and I could see no prospect of a qualified job later on without training, so I made my decision. Having filled in a Notice Paper with my personal details, including 'Trade or Calling', which I gave as 'Refrigeration Engineer's Assistant' and 'Qualifications' as 'School Certificate' and signed that I knew I was committing myself to three years regular service, I went home. As a prospective 'regular' I was allowed to take time for a holiday and to report to the Royal Air Force Reception Centre in August.

"I've signed on for three years," I announced, to my parents' surprise.

Early in August I reported, as instructed, to Bedford, using the Railway Warrant that had been sent to me. At the station a large number of us arriving for the same purpose were herded together and by means of lorries conveyed out to the Royal Air Force Station at Cardington in Bedfordshire, in the shadow of the great airship hangars, to be kitted out and enrolled.

The first shock was the discovery that I could only be an electrician if I signed on for a total of four years. The promise that had been made at the recruiting office was less than fully truthful. Certainly some trades could be pursued on a three-year engagement, and these included such attractions as canteen hands, fire-fighters and some menial occupations. It might have been worse; 'Electrical Mechanic Ground' was among the trades available on a four-year contract while others, presumed more skilled, required a minimum commitment of five years, which was an even greater shock to some of us.

Entering into discussion about the situation, I was assured that the proposed trade would involve training equivalent to that of an electrical mechanic in civilian life. After Initial Training I would attend a sixteen-week concentrated instruction course at a Trade Training School and become an electrician, competent in all areas of electrical theory and practice, with basic knowledge of wiring, standard equipment, repair procedures and so on, and be qualified to be accepted for employment in the profession upon my demobilisation. I would emerge from the training as an Aircraftman First Class and during my service career have opportunities for promotion to higher ranks, all carrying increases in pay.

"May I phone home and make a decision tomorrow?" I asked.

"No you may not. You must decide now."

In the evening I found a public kiosk and phoned home, an operation that necessitated calling a neighbour and asking him to fetch my father.

"How are you getting on?" he asked breathlessly when he arrived.

"Great! I'm signing on for a total of four years."

"Blimey!"

We were allocated a hut as temporary accommodation for the few days of our stay. Nearly all of us were eighteen and nearly all of us enduring communal life for the first time.

Most of us, I suspect, had led a fairly cosseted life and for some even the tasks of pressing clothes and cleaning shoes would be a new experience. Oh what a shock we were going to have! There were a few older men in their early twenties who had been able to defer entry and one really old fellow who had already been in the Navy and fancied regular Air Force life as a career. He must have been twenty-five if he was a day!

From the sea of anonymous faces, two stand out in memory. One belonged to a boy with a head in the shape of a perfect oval, with a tuft of coarse hair rising vertically above it to a point. We never knew his name but he was, with stunning originality, immediately christened 'coconut'. He informed us proudly that he came from Woffud, which, after he had elaborated on the delights of that mystical town, I realised was Watford. We took delight in teasing him about his mispronunciations; he couldn't, for instance, say the word 'vehicle', which he rendered as 'virical'.

The other young man was what we, in those different days, would have called a 'Nancy-boy'. You won't find much about homosexuality in these memoirs. Spurious statistics were bandied about and whenever a group of men assembled, someone would often comment mischievously, "It's supposed to be one-in-four. It's not me, so which of you three is it?" However, discovery or admission of such illegal tendencies would then have had very serious consequences, so these matters were kept quiet. With one exception, occurring at the end of my initial training, I went through four years of communal life without being conscious of anything of this nature.

It is not possible to say whether this particular recruit was gay but he was certainly affected. He arrived wearing clothes the like of which none of us had seen before. Normal best casual wear was a pair of grey flannel trousers and a tweed jacket, but his was brightly coloured and stylishly cut. His beautifully coiffured hair covered his ears and rested gently on his collar, which fact alone made him unique and the subject of much abuse. His expression suggested a tendency to burst into tears.

The first night was not uneventful. Installed in our large hut, one of a great number on the site, it was for some of us the first time that we had slept away from home. It was only five years since the war so a number of us had not even had a decent holiday, and there was a somewhat hysterical atmosphere. Having washed communally and undressed in public, both new experiences, we climbed into our iron-framed beds. I looked around me at my companions. They came from all walks of life and I knew nothing about them. Could they be trusted? Some of them looked decidedly 'sharp'. I took my wallet out of my jacket and slipped it under my pillow, and put my watch back on my wrist. Later I discovered that most of us had done the same, starting a habit that would be maintained throughout our service life. One of the boys, religiously brought up, knelt at his bedside, probably for the last time.

"Oi! Say one for me!"

"You won't find one under the bed; if you want a slash you'll have to go out the back."

Such ribaldry must have been considered to be of a high standard to judge by the nervous laughter it aroused. We put the light out but as we lay in our unfamiliar surroundings sleep would not come. One of the lads started giggling.

"Did you hear about the man who went into a chemist's and asked for 144 French Letters? (We didn't call them condoms then) He wanted to commit gross indecency!"

There were groans all round. After a pause another voice was heard in the darkness.

"Why do the postmen in France have Roman numerals on their hats?"

"Go on."

"Well they wouldn't want them to be French letters, would they?"

More vulgar stories followed until a figure appeared in the doorway. It was the sergeant responsible for us, who lived in a self-contained cubicle at the end of the hut.

"Every week I hope that someone's going to come up with a story I haven't heard," he grumbled, "so please go to sleep."

"Sorry sarge."

We did make an attempt but sleep still evaded us. Before long the nervy giggling and occasional bawdy jokes started up again, incurring the further wrath of the NCO.

"Sorry sarge, we'll be good."

And, with considerable restraint, we were. Soon all that could be heard was the gentle sobbing of the effeminate young man crying himself to sleep and eventually we all drifted off. Sometime in the night I awoke with a scream, wondering what had happened and where I was. Where I was, actually, was on the floor! I had fallen out of bed in my sleep. The bed was considerably narrower than my own at home and the blankets provided were hardly wider than the bed. At that point I adopted another habit, which I continued for the next four years, of laying the blankets across the bed sideways so that they could tuck under the mattress.

In no time at all the sergeant was waking us up. He was a kindly man, that sergeant. In the mornings he would enter the hut bearing a bucket of steaming tea in which we dipped our mugs.

The short time we spent at Cardington was well filled. Firstly we were allocated our service numbers. Mine was 4076503 or 503 for short. It's true that you never forget it.

A major undertaking was 'kitting out'. In a large warehouse we were handed clothing of very approximately the right size, including Working Blue (a uniform of battledress style for every-day use), Best Blue (a suit cut more stylishly with fuller-length jacket and brass buttons, for use on parades, official occasions and excursions beyond the camp gates), braces, collars, ties, socks, pyjamas, towels, pullovers, gloves, shorts and vests for physical training, boots, shoes and a greatcoat. We had seen regular airmen about the place wearing the rather stylish forage caps but these were being phased out and we were handed dreadful shapeless berets with brass cap badges to put in them.

There were a number of items of webbing material such as belts, cross straps, bayonet frogs and large and small packs, and certain items of hardware such as button-sticks, brushes, forks, spoons and mugs. Also there were large and small rectangular mess tins made of aluminium. These last two items were carried about the world by all of us and never used as there was always a mess hall with proper crockery wherever we went.

A kit-bag was provided to contain all of the stuff that you weren't actually wearing. Virtually all of this kit had to be identified with one's service number. For the clothing, where possible, this was done by means of a stamp made up with blocks like an oversized John Bull printing outfit, (remember them?) and a black impression was made on shirt tails, collars and so on. Smaller labels were provided for attaching to other items. Once this was done and the uniform on, we were instructed to make a parcel up of all our civilian clothing and post it off home.

"Aren't we allowed to keep our own clothes?"

"Not until after your square-bashing; that is the next eight weeks. When you get your next posting you will be allowed locker space for private possessions."

So much scrounging went on to find scraps of brown paper and string, or to buy them from the NAAFI, followed by a call at the camp post office.

A visit to the camp barber was compulsory however much anyone protested that his hair had recently been cut. We were speedily given the standard service short-back- and-sides which seemed to be designed to conceal all natural growth from the world once the beret was in place. Acres of pink flesh right up the backs of necks saw light for the first time. The nice young man, who had nearly given way to his emotions upon his treasured apparel being replaced by rough uniform, burst into tears as his luxuriant locks fell away. Perhaps, I thought, he'll suffer less in the weeks to come from our coarse insults now that he looks more like the rest of us.

Possession of a uniform and smart appearance meant that we could now be photographed. Wearing the obligatory criminal expression we had mug shots taken which turned up later attached to small pieces of paste board that were our identity cards. These were form number 1250, known universally as a 'twelve-fifty'. The penalty for losing one, it seemed, was too severe to contemplate. We looked at each other. In the regulation blue serge battledress we had now lost our individuality to a uniform appearance. There were no badges of rank or other qualifications on our sleeves yet, just the flashes of a bird in flight on each shoulder.

"What is it, a sparrow?" someone asked.

"Probably an albatross."

"Why are they facing backwards?"

"Probably an indication that we are in for a tough time, struggling to keep going forward."

We were ushered into a lecture hut to see the pox film. Before the pox film we got the pox lecture from a member of the medical staff.

"Now that your mummies and daddies have let you libidinous lot loose on the world I hope that they warned you about dirty women. Now, they probably think that their little darlings wouldn't get up to anything unsavoury, but you are about to embark on a predominately male existence, cut off from your nearest and dearest and if you've got anything in your veins you will get urges. Wherever servicemen find themselves there will never be a shortage of willing ladies anxious to satisfy, freely or for a consideration, their lascivious appetites. And don't be taken in by appearances. Even the most demure girl, if she's willing, will be offering you a route taken by many before. The result of this promiscuity is frequently unfortunate. What am I talking about? VD. Venereal diseases. That's what I'm talking about. Now there are several of them, the most common being syphilis and gonorrhoea and they're all 'orrible, causing various very unpleasant sorts of knob-rot. The best advice is to leave women alone and save yourselves for your loved-ones at home. If you're hell-bent on adventure, contraceptives are available, for your benefit, not for theirs, and if you just have to have an unprotected dabble, report immediately afterwards for belated prophylactic treatment. If you do develop any abnormalities in your hitherto pristine parts you must report them at once. The cures are nasty but the diseases are worse. You will be given regular medical inspections on the state of your equipment. Now we'll see the film..."

The lights were put out and the epic started. The first part echoed the dire warnings that we had been given, the causes, effects and treatment of the various conditions being covered in a more comprehensive and professional manner. The rest of the film was taken up with a great number of individual cases, being a succession of close-ups of male genitalia in various stages of the different diseases that could affect them, exhibiting great sores, blisters and wounds, and an indication of the severity and longevity of treatments that were available. All this was depicted in glorious colour. As an exercise in morality the film was an effective deterrent. AIDS hadn't been invented then but VD seemed bad enough.

The lights went on. Several faces were pale.

"Any questions?" asked the medico.

"Do we get to see the film they show the WRAFs?" (Women's Royal Air Force, i.e. girls).

"Any *sensible* questions?"

A short embarrassed silence ensued.

"Is it true you can catch VD from a lavatory seat?"

"Is that what your dad told your mum? No, son, you only get it from inserting yourself into places where it's best not to. There are just two people who can get it from a lavatory seat," he grinned, "and that's the padre and me!"

For many of us all this alarming information was academic. There was a lot of virginity about in the 1950s, owing to the moral climate, good upbringing, fear of pregnancy and the fact that many young men were completely tongue-tied in the presence of the opposite sex.

The most significant event during those few days was the Attestation. The Notice Paper detailed conditions of enlistment such as an obligation to serve anywhere in the world and work anywhere required, ashore or afloat or in the air, and the serious penalties for not doing anything that anyone told you to do. It advised us that within three months we could pay a sum not exceeding £20 "for the use of His Majesty" and be discharged if we wished. Presumably we would still have had to complete a statutory two years National Service period anyway so I don't suppose that His Majesty made much use of that source of income. A number of further questions on the Notice Paper had to be answered, some of a personal nature beginning "do you understand that..." reinforcing the conditions relating to service in the

Royal Air Force. The question that a number of us hesitated over related to Religious Denomination. There appeared to be only three categories permitted, namely Church of England, Roman Catholic and Other Denominations. And, no, we were told, there are no Atheists or Agnostics in the Royal Air Force; any clever dick disposed to claim these descriptions, possibly to avoid attending functions such as Church Parades, was promptly classified as "C of E" or "O.D."

Having indicated that I had obtained the School Certificate it was pointed out to me that this carried an advantage. "When, in due course," I was told, "you sit for and pass trade examinations entitling you to higher rank, you can only be promoted if you also have a certain level of education. For many of you this means that you will have to study for and sit the Air Force's Examination of General Education as well as the one in your special technical subject. The School Certificate is accepted as evidence of at least equal education and means that you will get any trade promotions as soon as you pass in them. You will be moving on from here very soon so when you get to your next camp, write home, get your School Certificate sent to you and get it recorded on your service records."

Having answered all the questions we signed a declaration of accuracy. I was a little alarmed to notice that I was signing on for a term of five and a half years until I realised that this consisted of four years regular service plus eighteen months after demobilisation transferred to 'Class E of the Reserve', a period of normal civilian life subject to the possibility of recall 'in defence of the United kingdom against actual or apprehended attack, or when warlike operations are in preparation or in progress'.

I then took the oath:-

"I, Raymond Lewis Clinton, swear by Almighty God that I will be faithful and bear true allegiance to His

Majesty King George the Sixth, His Heirs and Succes-
sors, and that I will, as in duty bound, honestly and
faithfully defend His Majesty, His Heirs and Successors,
in Person, Crown and Dignity against all enemies and
will observe and obey all orders of His Majesty, His Heirs
and Successors, and of the Air Officers and Officers set
over me. So help me God."

An Attesting Officer signed the Notice Paper confirming that I had understood and answered accordingly all the questions and that I had taken the oath.. He dated it; the 9th day of August 1951. I was now an airman. I wasn't much of one; I was an 'Aircraftman 2nd Class' or AC2, the lowest form of life on the planet.

Along with my new acquaintances I was informed that I was posted to No.1 School of Recruit Training, Royal Air Force, Henlow.

"Where the hell's Henlow?" someone asked. "Right at the other end of the country, no doubt."

"No I don't think so," I replied, the name striking some sort of chord. "I believe you'll find its somewhere in this area."

We were assembled and ambled off through the camp with our new belongings stuffed into our kit-bags, which were balanced precariously across one shoulder. The kit-bag, incidentally, was the daftest piece of luggage ever invented and quite incapable of being carried easily. It was a canvas cylinder with an opening at one end that was fastened with a length of rope that also served as a handle. Upright, it stood too tall to be carried in the hand and horizontal on one shoulder it was so wide that in this required position it was necessary to bend the neck awkwardly and lean to one side. Even the addition of a handle or strap half-way down the side would have made life easier. Any article that you needed would, of course, be buried at the bottom.

I say "ambled" advisedly, as what we were doing in no way resembled marching. We still had to learn how to do that. Expecting to be loaded into trucks for transportation to Bedford railway station or our destination, we were instead, rather to our surprise, led across open land to a waiting train standing on a branch line passing right through the site. The train trundled a few miles across country and deposited us right alongside the main gate of the School of Training.

Heaving our kit-bags up again, we staggered into the camp and were kept on the move for a considerable distance past endless rows of wooden huts stretching to the horizon in all directions. At last someone shouted "HALT" and with relief we eased the heavy loads off our aching shoulders and dumped them on the ground.

2.   Square-bashing

"AS YOU WERE! AS YOU WERE! No-one told you to lower those kit-bags. Get them back up on your shoulders. MOVE! You're not at Cardington Holiday Camp now! Here at Henlow you obey instructions, not think for yourselves. NOT THINK FOR YOURSELVES!"

We were surrounded by a number of loud aggressive young men bearing the two stripes on their sleeves that identified the rank of corporal, all immaculately dressed with uniforms pressed, well-creased trousers neatly tucked into gaiters and boots you could see your face in. Everywhere they went they marched with erect military bearing and everything they said to us was communicated in a shout. In a disorganised manner we got the kit-bags up again, painfully.

"Lower kit-bags! TOGETHER! TOGETHER! Raise them again. Now lower kit-bags. Raise-kit bags. Lower kit-bags." We eased our aching shoulders.

"And STAND STILL until you're told to Stand Easy. Stand at ... Ease! Stand Easy! Now, you're here for eight weeks during which time we've got the almost impossible task of turning you into proper airmen. At the moment you are nothing more than a SHOWER!"

The corporal approached one of us at random and bellowed at him from a distance of about six inches.

"YOU'RE A SHOWER! A SHOWER OF SHIT! What are you?"

"Er, a shower?"

"A shower of shit! What are you?"

"A shower of shit."

"A shower of shit, CORPORAL!"

"A shower of shit, corporal."

" Now double into a hut, pick yourselves a bed, dump your kit onto it and double back here."

We did that and took up position again, roughly in rank and file.

"Atten ... SHUN! Stand at ... EASE! Atten ... SHUN! Stand at ... EASE! Terrible! Now, you lot are a 'Flight', Heaven help us! You one hundred dregs of humanity are 'Flight 2A'. You've already got off to a bad start; you walked on the hut floor." We looked at each other in bewilderment.

"Stand still and no talking in the ranks! You may have noticed that everything in your quarters is spotlessly clean, including the highly-polished lino floor ... and it's going to stay that way. By the door as you go in you will find a pile of felt squares. You take two and you slide on them all the time that you are wearing boots. While you are here you take your orders from us, and if you disobey any of us you will find yourself ON A CHARGE, with dire consequences. Any complaints, you bring to us, and don't think you can by-pass us and go moaning about us to someone higher because, as they will tell you, they only accept representations approved by us, and WE decide whether your complaint justifies worrying a busy officer.

Right then, we'd better start by trying to make you look like airmen. Have you any idea what you look like? First, your berets; they are like sacks stuck on your heads. Get the head-band parallel with your eyebrows, cap-badge over the left eye and with the waste material pulled down to the right."

So it continued.

"If at any time you fail in performance or appearance you are liable to be RE-FLIGHTED; that is put down into a later Flight and have to stay here a bit longer. Is that all understood?"

"Er, yes."

"Yes, CORPORAL."

"Yes, corporal."

And that was the rude introduction to our Drill Instructors, the tin gods who controlled every aspect of our existence for every moment of the next two months.

There were several facts that we did not realise for some time. These men were mostly no more than boys themselves. They were in authority over us through having chosen 'Drill Instructor' as their service occupation and had undergone the appropriate training period. Several of them had therefore only a few weeks more service behind them than us. Furthermore, most of them were not really corporals at all, holding that 'acting' rank in view of the role they were playing. Nevertheless, their dominance over us was absolute.

The philosophy of the training was never explained to us at the time; military persons on active service, and no-one could say what we might be called on to do later, must obey all orders at all times unquestioningly. Our individuality had to be brainwashed out of us until, upon the command "jump", we would jump without querying whatever it was we might be jumping into. Of course, at the same time we had to become expert at marching and drill and uphold the smart tradition of the service when in the public eye. Initial Training was not known as square-bashing for nothing.

Accommodation was in wooden huts, a number arranged like ribs attached to a spine. The 'spine' was a long narrow 'ablutions' area containing rows of washbasins, showers, urinals and WCs and the huts were spread out on either side, each connected to it by a short, covered walkway. This arrangement was repeated throughout the accommodation area. Each airman had a bed-space on which stood an iron bedstead with mattress and a tall wardrobe or locker. In the centre of the room were long wooden racks for stacking our rifles and on the floor, laid out in symmetrical pattern, the brooms, buffers and other cleaning utensils. A private cubicle at one end of the hut was the living quarters of one of the Drill Instructors, who was soon out telling us what to do. His first action was to collect from each of us a sum of money as 'Barrack Damages' to cover, apparently, the cost of replacing anything we might damage during our stay.

One side of each locker was for a greatcoat and whichever 'blue' was not being worn. There were no hangers; we were directed to the NAAFI shop to purchase these. Needless to say, everything was going to be inspected critically the following morning. It was the other side of the locker that proved the most problematical. It consisted of shelving that created a series of square, open-fronted boxes, some of which were for the rest of our clothing. This had to be arranged in specific order: blue PT shorts alternating with white tops, then shirts and underwear, ending with socks at the top. These all had to fill the space evenly and completely, presenting a flat face as if pressed up against glass. This was achieved by cutting out cardboard (acquired by another trip to the NAAFI) to the precise width required, scoring it and folding it in strips inside the various garments, an operation performed several times a day, with some difficulty.

Behind this façade went dirty clothing awaiting laundry and personal possessions, which were probably only writing materials and sponge bags. As a matter of course, a passing corporal would regularly take exception to one or more of these assemblies and poke it in with his drill stick. Reassembly usually meant being late on parade, incurring much abuse and threats of punishment, with the possibility of rushing down the hut at such speed that a foot slipped off the felt pad and a stud scraped the floor.

There was, naturally, a procedure for the blankets and sheets, which had to be folded in a neat pile, with one blanket around them to create a perfect boxed effect at the head of the bed. On the bed, throughout the working day, a number of articles had to be displayed neatly for inspection, including brushes for boots, clothes and blanco, and one's own safety razor. I discovered one evening that my razor was missing. Having already learned that the standard reply to "Corporal, part of my kit has been nicked," was "Nick someone else's then," I did not think that this would apply to an item connected with personal toiletry, so I ventured to approach authority.

"Please, corporal, I think my razor has been stolen."

"No it hasn't. It has been confiscated by me! It was FILTHAY! FILTHAY!"

"It isn't filthy, corporal, I rinse it every day, although I am aware that the chrome is wearing off to reveal the brass beneath. May I have it please? It is my personal property."

"You may not. It was disgusting and I have disposed of it. Get yourself a new one from the NAAFI shop."

Keeping personal appearance up to a required standard consumed a lot of our so-called 'off-duty' hours. Clothes had to be pressed and we took turns with the iron and ironing board, making well-defined creases in trousers. We soon discovered the benefit of pressing them with a damp cloth, followed by brown paper, after first applying soap to the insides of the creases. All the brass, such as buttons, cap-badges and buckles, had to be polished with Brasso or Duraglit, with the help of a button-stick and blanco (blue, not white) had to be applied on a regular basis to all webbing such as belt, straps and large or small packs. The large pack, often carrying the folded greatcoat, had to look completely flat on all sides, an effect achieved by scrounging plywood and constructing a box frame to fit inside tightly.

Shoes had to be highly polished, as did boots, which presented a particular problem. As issued, the boots were made all over of a rough-finished knobbly leather, but the toe-cap area had to acquire a smooth, shiny surface as quickly as possible. This was achieved by continual brushing and other means including spit and polish and smoothing with a toothbrush handle or the back of a spoon. In spite of all our efforts, no-one was ever deemed, at daily inspection, to be achieving the desired effect quickly enough and shortcuts to success were debated. Rumour suggested applying a thick layer of boot polish and setting it alight to melt the surface, so one chap tried it out. As we stood in a circle, watching the flames, a man entered the hut.

"What on earth are you doing?" he asked.

"Setting fire to our fucking kit," someone replied sarcastically, without looking round to see who it was.

It was the padre.

The Lee Enfield .303 rifle provided for each of us was inspected regularly. In its butt end was a concealed compartment containing a small square of material attached to a length of cord, known as a 'pull-through' and a small bottle of oil for cleaning the barrel and lubricating the bolt.

The NAAFI shop profited further from the provision of boot polish, Brasso, Blanco and dusters for all these activities, which mostly occupied our evening hours, and later from the regular necessities of razor blades, toothpaste and the obligatory Brylcreem.

In addition to the above, one evening a week was 'Bull Night', when the hut was completely cleaned. Beds were moved, the floor swept, covered in polish and finished off with a padded concrete buffer, the windows polished and all surfaces cleaned. Then all the utensils used had to be cleaned and replaced in their precise pattern on the floor. The grubby broom handles were scraped clean with a razor blade and were already dangerously thin in the middle.

The normal working day began with our corporal bellowing at us to wake and arise, snatching the bed clothes off anyone reluctant to comply. One morning this caught out one lad, apparently asleep with a smile on his face, who was, in fact, amusing himself.

Following ablutions we formed ranks outside and were marched to the Airmen's Mess for breakfast, clutching our 'eating irons' and mugs. Eating there was always a nauseating experience. The food, dispensed through hatches onto our plates as our queue passed by in cafeteria fashion, was invariably unsavoury. At lunchtime 'potato' was served. This re-constituted sticky substance normally defied all efforts and the law of gravity to make it leave the server's heavy-duty, long-handled spoon so he would knock it across another spoon to dislodge it. The heavy pellet of goo would hit the plate with such force that it almost knocked it out of your hand. Foul-tasting tea to accompany this feast was drawn from an enormous urn.

After a meal, taken at long trestles with benches, you scraped your leavings into a disgusting bin, which presumably was emptied occasionally, and dumped your plate on a pile. You then passed through an annexe to wash knife, fork, spoon and mug. The facility provided for this was a large galvanised tank of water, supposedly boiling but always nearly cold, on which floated a greasy scum of the residue from previous users. You dipped your irons in this and hoped for the best. An indefinable aroma, with elements of rotting vegetation and damp sacking, pervaded the whole building. All of this was more than I could stomach first thing and I took to missing the breakfast parade, a fact immediately noticed.

"Get on parade. I could put you on a CHARGE for this."

"But I really don't eat breakfast, corporal."

"I don't care what you eat but you will march to the mess and you will march back." So I did.

It was possible, fortunately, to supplement the diet at one's own expense during the evenings, if time could be found, by visiting the NAAFI canteen. The Navy, Army and Air Force Institutes runs canteens, bars and shops for service personnel and their families on all military camps, providing cafeteria facilities (with chips featuring prominently) and opportunities for social activities such as darts and snooker. Some sites also had a Salvation Army or 'Sally Ann' establishment along similar lines. For any spiritual needs inappropriate for a services padre officers of the Church Army were often to be seen.

After breakfast, having folded our sheets and blankets in the approved manner, erected our locker displays and swept and dusted our bed spaces, our regular daily routine started with an inspection parade. This was another opportunity to be insulted and threatened with punishment, with random investigations into supposed misdemeanours such as losing any of the thirteen studs in the soles of each boot.

"Am I hurting you, airman?"

"No corporal."

"Well I ought to be; I'm standing on your hair. Get it cut by tomorrow morning's parade."

These inspections took place twice daily. One afternoon I was accused of being unshaven.

"But I assure you, corporal, I did shave this morning."

"I repeat, you are unshaven. You have not shaved today."

"Yes I have, corporal."

"Well if it grows as quickly as that from now on you will shave before both morning and afternoon parades."

So I did, although finding the time was a nightmare.

A very large proportion of our working days throughout the eight weeks was spent on drill, mostly on the parade ground, a hallowed place that under no other circumstances could be used as a shortcut from one side to the other. Starting with basic forming of ranks, coming to 'attention', 'at ease' and 'easy' we progressed onto drill with the rifle. At the 'slope arms' this had to be supported across the left shoulder, with the left forearm parallel to the ground, a most uncomfortable position in which to bear its weight of nine pounds for any period. At about this time we were all vaccinated against smallpox, needless to say in the left arms, which were already stiff enough. We marched with our Drill Instructors at our side constantly shouting orders and chiding.

" 'eft! 'ight! 'eft! 'ight! About ... turn two three four! Open your legs in front; nothing will fall! Flight ... HALT! Order ... ARMS! Stand at ... EASE!" On that final command the rifle was thrust forward and inevitably someone let his clatter to the ground. The rest of us awaited developments.

"You fool; you cretin; you POLTROON! Malicious damage to armaments is a Court Martial offence."

"It wasn't malicious, corporal."

"SHUT UP! The next time you do that I shall take my drill stick, insert it into your anus and shove it until it emerges out of one of your nostrils. PICK IT UP!"

Most of us, having a sense of rhythm and a pride in the accomplishment, found the drill very satisfying. But there was always someone who couldn't start on the left foot (and 'by the right quick march' has nothing to do with feet but on dressing, which means keeping level with the person at your side) and who had not mastered the drill for changing step on the march. Some always put the same arms and legs forward, right arm and right leg and then left arm and leg. Then there were those uncoordinated individuals whose feet appeared to be in step but who somehow made their heads bob up and down out of time with the others. The threat of a charge hung over these individuals in particular but was rarely invoked. I doubt if it would have been legal. More likely they were kept back on parade for an hour of further training as punishment thus, quite possibly, missing a meal or being late on parade for the next period and frequently encroaching into precious evening hours. Other Flights, of more recent or longer service, shared the parade ground, each with their own Drill Instructors barking out commands and as the weeks went by it was obvious by comparison that we were becoming a smart well-drilled body of men (well, most of us).

We learned how to salute with the hand; long way up, short way down and with palms facing forward unlike the naval way; and with the rifle, in the 'slope arms' position. The snag was knowing when to do it. The only recipients of this courtesy were commissioned officers and at all times. On the principle of being on the safe side, when in doubt, to start with we saluted everything in a possibly appropriate uniform, including members of the Salvation Army, the Church Army, quite likely passing postmen and Warrant Officers, who dressed like officers but were, in fact, non-commissioned. Getting it wrong usually led to being ordered to halt for a reprimand.

There were breaks in the routine. We would be fallen out for a quick smoke – and in those days many appreciated this – and for longer NAAFI breaks for a 'tea and a wad', if you could get anywhere near the front of the queue before being summarily ordered back on parade. In authority over the instructors was a sergeant, an older man, who occasionally took some of the sessions.

"How long have you been in the raff, sarge?" one lad ventured to ask him during one of the tea breaks. He went quite red in the face.

"Firstly I'm not a 'sarge'. To you I am a sergeant, alright? Secondly I'm not in the raff, or even the riff-raff; I'm in the

Royal Air Force and so are you, so don't ever call it anything else!"

In the early days in particular, it was difficult for many of us to adapt so suddenly to this regime, so different from the cosseted life of a young man growing up in a cosy family atmosphere. Eight weeks does not seem long, looking back on it, but at the time, looking forward, the end seemed almost beyond reach. To be so completely under relentless authority for twenty-four hours a day, constantly insulted and punished, having little time of your own or anyone to turn to for help while feeling always weary was very hard. Too hard for some, who were at times near to tears and for one recruit who, prior to our arrival, it was rumoured, perhaps apocryphally, had committed suicide.

It was possible to leave camp after daytime activities but not easy. Having found the time, donned 'best blue' and shoes, and ensured that every aspect of one's appearance was perfect, it was necessary to present oneself for approval at the guardroom by the main gate. This was manned by daunting SPs or Station Police, in white belts and peaked caps and known as 'Snowdrops' They were fully paid-up members of the intimidation regime and had a number of jolly practices. On one occasion I had to remove my cap-badge to see if it was as well polished on the back as on the front and on another was accused of having dust in my welts.

"Dust in my *what*, corporal?"

"Your welts; where the sole of your shoe joins the upper." The guardroom was a walk of about a quarter of a mile from the hut, so this wasn't surprising. There was always about a fifty per cent chance of having to traipse back to the hut to rectify such offences before enjoying a taste of freedom in the big world outside. The choices were the nearby crossroads, on which stood a pub and a café or, a bus-ride away, the fleshpots of Hitchin. I did get to the cinema with some mates a couple of times and one weekend my parents borrowed a neighbour's car and travelled over to meet me in the local café. On the way back into camp you had to report again to the SPs, so you had to be within the permitted time limit, still smart, sober and well-behaved ... or else!

One evening our corporal emerged from his sanctum, looked around and bellowed "Now then, who takes size eight shoes? Come on! Come on!" After an uncomfortable pause one man volunteered that he did.

"Right. Mine are at the repairers so I'll borrow yours for my evening out." He must have marched as determinedly on his date as he did in his boots on parade for upon his return the borrowed shoes were worn right down at the heel and the owner was effectively confined to camp without best foot-wear while they too went to the repairer.

Somehow time was found for writing the all-important letters home. I had my School Certificate sent to me, got it entered on my records and posted it back home. Incoming mail was distributed, or I should say tossed in our general direction, publicly at daily parades.

"Smith 432."

"Corporal!"

"I see your parents are as illiterate as you are. Brown 897."

"Corporal!"

"Pink paper, Brown! And scented! She must love you, ugly as you are!"

Girlfriends would print coded messages on the flaps of the envelopes. "S.W.A.L.K." stood for "Sealed with a loving kiss" and "I.T.A.L.Y." for "I trust and love you". The boys would reply with "N.O.R.W.I.C.H.", which meant "(K)nickers off ready when I come home."

One day there was a departure from the normal routine. We were marched onto the parade ground together with the entire complement of personnel on the camp and formed up on all sides of a raised platform that had been erected in the centre. The Commanding Officer and other big-wigs mounted this followed by a corporal being marched on between two Air Force policemen. An officer addressed us.

"You are called upon to witness the carrying out of a sentence imposed by Court Martial upon Corporal xxxxxxxx. A clerk will read out the convictions."

"First charge; Corporal xxxxxxxx did, on the so-and-so day of such-and-such month, 1951, misappropriate monies entrusted to him for safe keeping." Further charges, totalling about fourteen, relating to the same offence on other dates, were read out. "Corporal xxxxxxxx, having been found guilty by Court Martial on all counts, was sentenced to be reduced to the ranks and ignominiously discharged from the Royal Air Force."

The first part of this punishment was effected by the corporal's stripes being ripped off his jacket, having been prepared for this by being tacked on loosely. For the Discharge we were all marched to the main gate where we formed up again in Flights. The unfortunate criminal was quite literally kicked through the gate and his suitcase was slung out after him. Later we learned the full story. He had been suggesting habitually to the men under his care that money would be safer entrusted to him during the times, such as Physical Training, when it had to be left in the hut. Subsequently he would deny any knowledge of this, relying on the powers of intimidation to block any complaint. Somehow someone had got round this, perhaps through the padre, and alerted the authorities.

These PT sessions, a regular interruption to our normal drill, were like being back in the school gym, involving ropes, vaulting horses and medicine balls. Each period usually finished with us on our haunches in single file, bouncing up and down and singing:

"Sons of the sea, bobbing up and down like this.
Sailing the ocean, bobbing up and down like this.
We'll build a ship my lads, bobbing up and down like
this.
Oh you can't beat the boys of FLIGHT 2A, bobbing up
and down like this!"

At intervals we would set off on a cross-country run, out of the camp and across several miles of rural Bedfordshire. It has to be admitted that, at the outset, I was overweight and not very fit and invariably I trailed at the back of the pack. Regularly we were halted and I was hauled to the front, theoretically so that, as the slowest runner, I could set the pace, but I would soon be overtaken by everyone else and the process started over again. By the end of Initial Training I had lost several stones and was healthier than I had ever been. Several times, while I was at Henlow, my uniform had to go to a tailor to be taken in. My greatcoat, though, always looked like an oversized sack.

The worst aspect of PT was probably the changes of clothing it entailed, all against the pressure of time and the shouted threats of the NCOs on the consequences of being, yet again, late on parade. The kit, vests, shorts and canvas shoes, had to be removed from the smart 'wall' in the locker which then had to be rebuilt. This had to be disturbed again on return from the gym to conceal the discarded items now awaiting laundry and re-built yet again. Changing back into 'working blue' took time, largely because of the difficulty of affixing, with front and back studs if you hadn't lost them, a separate shirt collar several sizes too small or too large. This resulted from the weekly procedure for laundry which was bundled up, labelled sent away and in due course returned freshly clean. For new recruits, most kit was in excellent condition to start with but, somewhere along the line, probably at the laundry, parts of it would be 'appropriated' and replaced. Back would come worn and much-darned socks and ill-fitting collars. We envied the Army; they sensibly wore shirts with attached collars. On the other hand, so we were led to believe, they didn't get pyjamas.

One lad, running late, saved time by secreting his used gym kit under the mattress to avoid disturbing the locker display. It was discovered and he was actually put on a charge. This involved being marched in front of an officer and his misdemeanours recited, ending with "... prejudicial to good order and discipline and in default of King's Regulations." As 'KRs' incorporated a provision covering anything that anyone in superior position may order to be done, there was nothing for which you might not be charged. The officer would listen to anything that you wished to say, ignore it and pass sentence, in this case three days' CC or Confined to Camp, or in the vernacular 'Jankers'. During this period the offender had to report to the guardroom half-a-dozen times a day in full kit, including webbing and packs, fully 'bulled-up' for inspection and in the evening put in a spell of labour, normally in the mess kitchen. Fitting this in with an already pressurised existence was indeed a punishment.

There were facets of military service to be absorbed from various instructors, including familiarity with weaponry.

"Now then lads, this is a Mills bomb or, more familiarly, a hand grenade. You notice it is segmented. Why is it segmented?"

"We don't know, sergeant."

"Same as chocolate... so that everybody gets a piece."

We learned all there was to know about the workings of the Lee Enfield .303 rifle and the Bren and Sten automatic guns before ending up on the rifle range, a modest twenty-five yard affair with the customary red flag on a pole showing when it was in use. Properly maintained and accurate rifles were drawn from the armoury and for the first time we handled live rounds of ammunition. In batches, we lay prone and blew the hell out of the cardboard enemy, pulling the rifle butt well into the shoulder to avoid the recoil dislocating it. One airman, very likely the one who couldn't march in time, couldn't close only one eye in order to aim. It was either both open or both shut and the NCO in charge had to wedge a duster under his cap to obscure one eye.

Then came the Bren gun, under strict orders to fire it only in short bursts and finally the Sten, an ineffective-looking thing that seemed to have been welded together from bits of scrap metal and which was, apparently, much liable to jamming. This was fired in the standing position and again strictly in short bursts as it had a tendency otherwise to pull to the right and upwards. The non-blinking non-marcher panicked and kept his finger on the trigger. Everyone fell flat to the ground and watched the line of fire, which finally reached the flag-pole and cut it in half.

In order to train for any close combat in which we might, by some stretch of the imagination, be called upon to in-dulge in the future, we practised bayonet charging. The bayonets issued to us for this purpose and for the daily drill exercises were not the familiar flat blades used ceremonially but narrow, round-bladed spikes, tapering to a sharp point. With these fixed to the rifle barrel we would run at a stuffed sack, uttering blood-curdling screams, plunge the bayonet into it, then withdraw, shouting "In! Out! On guard!" and run past it to the next supposed enemy. This was all a bit mystifying as it seemed to assume that a foe would stand still uncomplainingly and permit such an assault to take place.

On another occasion we all donned respirators to experi-ence conditions under gas attack, in a sealed chamber.

The one activity to which I was not looking forward was the morning to be spent on the assault course, a large area at the back of the camp covered in tunnels, high walls, barbed wire, ropes over water to swing from and other forms of torture. This had to be negotiated under active conditions with instructors lobbing thunder flashes up tunnels behind you and firing rounds, hopefully blanks, over your heads. I knew that my rope-climbing and wall-scaling inabilities would result in humiliation but, as it happened, I was spared this ordeal. The reason for this was that on the morning in question it was my turn to act as Billet Orderly. Each airman was responsible on a daily basis for sweeping the dust and rubbish from his bed-space into the centre of the room. The Billet Orderly stayed behind to get the hut into tip-top condition. He swept up all the dirt and cleaned the windows and sills. He dusted the rifle racks, straightened all the rifles and laid the brooms and dustpans in their orderly arrangement on the floor. With a long piece of string he aligned all the beds and checked that individual kit displays were presentable. In short he virtually spring-cleaned the hut in readiness for the Orderly Officer, to whom he reported that the hut was ready for inspection.

On my morning I did all this and thought with some satisfaction that the place looked pretty good. I stood with a duster in my hand, not wishing to be accused of being idle, awaiting the visitation. Saluting with the other I said "Good morning sir; hut ready for your inspection."

"Hardly, is it, if you're still dusting?" They loved that sort of thing. The Orderly Sergeant stood behind him, notebook and pencil at the ready. Paying no attention to the fruits of all my labours, the officer bent down. The base plate of the rifle racks was a long wooden plank about a foot wide and mounted on slats at intervals so that it stood some half an inch off the floor. He poked his little stick under this. I nearly fainted. Out came a used and dirty cigarette packet! To my relief and surprise I heard no more about this; I imagine it was a daily occurrence and that my discomfiture may have been deemed sufficient punishment.

The anniversary of the Battle of Britain was celebrated throughout the Royal Air Force in the middle of September, when all flying stations were opened to the public for general interest and any sideshows, displays or other events that could be arranged. The School of Recruit Training was only one of several self-contained units at Henlow; next door was a small airfield that was laying on various amusements for the public and a few of us were detailed to assist in this. Two of us helped by selling tickets throughout the day for a competition that involved people estimating the altitude of a small 'plane which was circling overhead. It was not very onerous work so we expected no reward or even any expression of gratitude but someone in charge told us that in return for our help we could each have a short flight. Having never flown before, I found myself about to take my first trip – in a Tiger Moth. These wonderful old biplanes had such lift and gliding ability that it was alleged they could land themselves if the pilot passed out. I was handed a parachute.

"You're not going high enough to use it but you need it to be able to sit in the bucket seat, which is designed to accommodate it," I was told.

Strapped into this contraption, with the large square bulk of it suspended below the backside, I climbed into the open front cockpit. The pilot, already on board, flew the machine from the rear cockpit, the dual controls before me mimicking his movements. There was a slight wind and, at not much more than running pace, we were up.

The experience was exhilarating, like riding a motorbike in the sky. The wire struts between the wings twanged away in the airstream and it all seemed rather primitive, the fuel pipe from the tank overhead snaking down in spirals towards the engine. We made several circuits over the camp area – at some speed with the wind behind us but a great deal slower against it – and soon touched down again on the grass runway. One of the better days!

Periodically a full kit inspection took place, when virtually one's entire possessions had to be laid out on the bed with perfect symmetry to a regulation pattern, all items being in pristine condition.

"Stand by your beds!" Came the dreaded command.

Each man's display was inspected critically. If it failed to pass muster the whole bed would be tipped over unceremoniously and its entire contents, bed-clothes included, would have to be reassembled, with any sins rectified.

Another inspection, mercifully not too frequent, was the FFI, which stood for 'Free From Infection' – an embarrassing examination of one's private parts, conducted publicly. It was 'Stand by your beds' again, this time with trousers dropped to facilitate the Medical Officer's scrutiny, which sometimes entailed the use of his little stick to lift certain anatomical appendages.

As the end of our Initial Training approached our deportment and drill had improved out of all recognition and the demeanour of our instructors mellowed to the point where insults and criticism were sometimes replaced with encouragement and pride.

"Keep this up now, lads. We'll show them which is the best Flight on parade."

With perfect precision we could now form up on parade, 'tallest on the right; shortest on the left', breaking into a body of men whose heights rose in increments from the centre to the ends, and then dressing to the right with the arm extended to the next man's shoulder until it was slammed down in perfect unison upon the command "Eyes FRONT!" With heads erect and 'thumbs in line with the seams of the trousers' we stood at attention before performing all manner of drill movements. We marched, with arms consistently elevating to the correct angle, about-turned, halted and marked time with the knees reaching a uniform height. With the rifle we sloped, ordered and presented arms and performed the drill of extracting the bayonet from its 'frog' and 'fixing' it. At the 'slope' we marched across the parade ground in various configurations in both quick and slow time, with the right palm slapping across the rifle in salute, and carried out many other exercises of a similar nature. All of these actions we now performed upon a single command without either the instructor or ourselves shouting "one, two, three" at the intermediate stages. In short, we were as smart a bunch of servicemen as could be expected from a concentrated course of training. We posed for the official Flight souvenir photograph, which shows us smartly attired in 'best blue' and smiling broadly.

The big day came for our Passing-out Parade, complete with military band to complement the demonstration of our skills before the 'top brass' on the saluting dais, which we carried out with a feeling of some satisfaction. This meant that we had completed our Initial Training but it did not mean that we could depart from the school yet.

For one week we were transferred to Pool Flight. This was a system whereby all of the various units at Henlow could constantly be provided with a pool of labour to undertake the assorted chores and general maintenance necessary to keep a large establishment ticking over. I seemed to spend most of my time on a dust cart, collecting rubbish from the accommodation area and swill from the various mess halls and disposing of it at a dump. Each morning we reported to the corporal in charge of these arrangements in his small cubicle. He was as dissimilar from the other non-commissioned officers that we had encountered as could be imagined, being a much older man, probably in his forties.

He was a chubby, genial character, very friendly in manner. Much more friendly, in fact, than is customary between persons of the same sex and our suspicions were aroused.

Suddenly he said, "Ooh, I had a lovely girl last night and I'm still a bit sore," and dropped his trousers. "Look at that!"

'That' had a bandage round it.

"Yes, lovely she was but a virgin and a bit tight." Nobody believed him and we gave him a wide berth. Someone asked him how long he had been a corporal.

"Oh I've been more than that; twice I reached the appointment of sergeant but had to take on the lower rank again." This chequered career seemed to confirm our suspicions of an unorthodox and illegal (in those days) existence.

At the end of this period we were given our postings, to be taken up after a week's leave. The prospective electricians were to report to the School of Trade Training at Royal Air Force Melksham in Wiltshire and railway warrants were issued for travel home and the subsequent journey to our new postings. One of the final requirements was to fork out a sum of money for Barrack Damages.

"But we paid that at the beginning!"

"Well you have to pay it again. I expect you've done a lot more damage between you."

Of course, we hadn't done any; it was certainly a nice little racket on the part of the Drill Instructors.

How strange it was to be, once again, in the bosom of one's family, wearing civilian clothes, without separate collars and studs, and to have some leisure time at last. And how odd to adjust to the privilege of being able to think and make decisions of one's own. Acquaintance was re-established with my relations and friends.

"Hello!" they said. "When are you going back?"

RAF Henlow – No.1 School of Recruit Training.

After Square Bashing.

Before Square Bashing.

Snake Pass, on my bike.

Buxton Hotel (I don't know who the lady is).

With Pat, a Warrant Officer's daughter

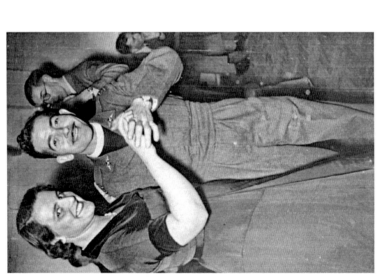

Padre and Mrs. Bennett.

A camp dance at RAF St Athan.

St Athan Christian Fellowship (I am on the left of the second row down).

Making scenery for a sketch.

The Coronation: ceremonial arch over The Mall and part of Selfridge's tribute.

In transit at Malta, getting used to our tropical kit.

Ship on the Suez Canal.

On the Canal Road, on a borrowed bike.

"Ablution" arrangements!

In full tropical kit, for "jankers".

Christmas 1953 in the tent.

Re-planning our tent!

With local traders.

Special treat; a day trip to Cairo.

In the Charging Room.

By the workshop.

Hotel "Ver de Luna," Nicosia.

Hotel "Florida", Famagusta.

A village street in Cyprus.

Sailing in Kyrenia harbour with Wendy.

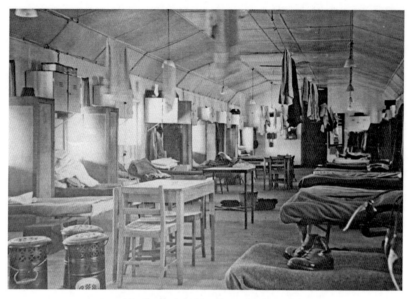

Inside the barrack block at RAF Abyad.

My 'bed-space' – with home-made table.

Army "trials" on the hill overlooking RAF Abyad.

An oasis on Abyad camp.

3.   RAF Melksham

In layout and general appearance, Royal Air Force Melksham was similar to Henlow. There were rows of huts connected to ablution areas, a guard room with its complement of Station Police, a mess or 'cook-house', a NAAFI and assorted other wooden buildings and hangars surrounding a large square or parade ground. In all other respects it was very different. It was a School of Training, of course, and there was still a bit more attention to discipline than we would later come to expect once we arrived at our operational postings, but it was fairly civilised. In the barracks we were permitted to have our civilian clothes and other personal effects with us, kept in lockers provided. Out of working hours, apart from periodic inspections, the weekly 'bull nights' and any responsibilities such as guard duty, we were largely left to our own devices.

We queued up at Stores to draw our bedding and were each issued with a 'Permanent Pass', which we had to show to get out of camp at all times. The drawback was that it could be taken away from you as punishment for any minor misdemeanour, as I soon discovered. We were woken each morning by music played over the Tannoy system and it was always the same record, popular at the time, of a song with a great deal of 'echo' effect which sounded quite eerie and soporific as you struggled into consciousness.

> *Good morning (morning, morning)*
> *Mister Echo (echo, echo, echo)*
> *How (how) are you (you) today (today, today, today)?*

I have always been slow to wake and too often I drifted back to sleep. The next thing I would know would be the

NCO standing over me and demanding my permanent pass, to be retrieved from the Squadron Office after an interval of one or two days.

It became evident that we were a cross-section of the population from areas right across the United Kingdom, with accents emanating from the North, the South, the South-west, the North-east, Wales and Scotland. Strange as it seems now, this was something of a novelty. There was not so much widespread travel then, either for leisure or business, and the BBC ensured that the radio waves carried only voices speaking Standard Pronunciation (i.e. posh Southern). We were consequently a mixed lot and from different backgrounds.

The man using the bed next to mine was certainly unconventional. He had decided that the easiest and quickest way to get on breakfast parade properly dressed was not to be very undressed the night before, and would get into bed wearing his underclothes, shirt and socks. His trousers and collar, with the tie already inserted and loosely knotted, lay on the chair beside him. At intervals we would frog-march him into the showers and insist on a change of clothing.

We embarked on our sixteen-week course in various huts got up as classrooms. Some of the time was spent on general subjects, useful for all but of particular benefit for those who would later be needing to sit the Air Force Examination of General Education for promotion.

"Good morning," said the Flying Officer who was our English tutor.

"Er, Good morning sir," we chanted, not knowing any better.

"I am not a sir, as I hope you have noticed. I am a WRAF officer and should be addressed as 'ma'am.'"

"Yes ma'am."

Regular religious periods proved more interesting than they might have been. Few of us concentrated on the padre's deep and meaningful homilies but he did show us some fascinating natural history films, the general idea of which seemed to be "Nature is wonderful, isn't it? God made all that, you know." The padre used to disappear into a projection box and work the machine himself. He wasn't very expert and the sound would frequently be out of synchronisation or the picture out of focus. He got it jammed completely once and with glee we watched on the screen the magnified image of the lamp slowly turning the film brown and finally setting fire to it.

Visits to the gym continued to keep us fighting fit but obviously the main purpose of the course was to teach us our trade. So with training in the technicalities of basic electrical theory and practice, interspersed with other subjects, it was much like being back at school. We reported to various classrooms or workshops for lessons, indulging in such mature activities as throwing chalk at each other while awaiting the arrival of the tutor. In one corner of our main classroom stood an old and dilapidated plywood 'Link Trainer'. This was, at a very fundamental level, the precursor of the Flight Simulator. When connected to a power supply it would swing round, tilt and bank in response to movements of the controls, to give some idea of the sensation of controlling a flying machine. Seated in the high-sided cockpit you were out of sight and we invariably indulged in a sort of Russian Roulette by taking it in turns to climb into it briefly and not be the one who sheepishly had to emerge and descend when the tutor arrived.

To give some idea of the trade training we received, I quote from the job specification given in my Certificate of Service, a document, incidentally, that I didn't see until the day I was 'demobbed':

> "Operates and performs routine inspections and elementary servicing on:- (a) Airfield Ground electrical

equipment, (b) Electrical components in the ground workshops, etc., (c) Electrical synthetic training devices. On this equipment, inspects wiring, switches etc., checks circuits for electrical leakage, continuity and resistance; diagnoses simple faults; rectifies minor defects; makes simple functional checks using simple electrical measuring instruments and standard test equipment. Operates battery charging equipment. Makes simple adjustments and replacements. Repairs defective cable connections and wiring harnesses. Cleans and lubricates parts. Packs components for transit. In addition, performs more complicated servicing or overhaul tasks on one particular ground installation or major item of ground electrical equipment. (Goodness knows what that meant!) May be employed in repair work on this range of work and, in addition, when qualified, on electro-plating duties."

It's all rather 'routine' and 'simple' isn't it? I most remember two particular subjects, so some time must have been spent on them. One was the function and repair of the 'Kent Clear Screen', a revolving transparent disc let into a windscreen to provide uninterrupted vision and used on boats. But when were we going to encounter boats? The other involved the intricacies of battery charging and in particular the dangers of diluting concentrated sulphuric acid down to a working solution, an operation involving special procedures and protective clothing. All of this was fully detailed in Poster 20, a document that had, by King's Regulations, to be displayed in all Battery Charging Rooms.

Our accommodation had to be kept in reasonably good order with regular cleaning sessions but at least we were allowed to walk on the floor! In order that we should not become rusty in the matters of drill and appearance there was still a morning parade before marching to school and some Church Parades on the parade ground prior to the C-of-Es and RCs marching off to their respective services. I never knew where the Other Denominations went. Inspections on these occasions were not very severe and presented no serious problem to any of us except one poor individual. Invariably the inspecting NCO would come to a halt behind him.

"Good God, man! Get your bleedin' 'air cut!"

"I can't, sergeant,"

"Don't you answer me back! Get it cut!"

"I can't, sergeant," followed by some muttering.

"It's a what?"

"It's a wig, sergeant."

"Sorry, lad. Carry on!"

It was too, and not a very good one. And bright red. A lot of fun was had with that hairpiece. Self-consciously the owner would go to sleep wearing it but in the morning it would have to be retrieved from other locations. I'm sure it would have been kinder for him to have been excused military service. Communal life was fun for a lot of men, an embarrassing nuisance for some and absolute purgatory for a few, mostly because of the endless joking and unkind practices. A good jape was to wait until someone was asleep and then wake him up and ask "Do you want to buy a battleship?" The retaliation was to wait until the perpetrator had dropped off then rouse him with the question, "What colour?"

Clever stuff, isn't it?

There was inevitably an individual selected for regular torment, largely on the grounds of his gullibility. You could tell him anything – from fictitious demands to report to the guardroom to the necessity of parading in the wrong uniform – and he would believe it and act accordingly every time. For no apparent reason, one night four chaps lifted his bed up, with him fast asleep in it, and gently lodged it between two rafters in the roof space. Having woken suddenly he got himself down but no-one would help him with the bed, which he eventually pushed down, taking a corner off the chest of drawers below.

'Barrack Damages' would cover that, no doubt.

Less deliberate but equally offensive were the antics of the late-night revellers returning from local hostelries, always rowdy and occasionally incapable. It is not very sociable to roll into the hut, wake everybody up and urinate all over someone in bed. One Lothario, patently sober, returned late at night with his clothes saturated and smelling vilely.

"I persuaded this girl to come into a barn with me. We were just getting down to the business, in the pitch black, when we heard someone come in so we froze. He only wanted a quick piss, which he did right over us!"

Oh, the joys of a communal existence!

Sometimes persistent unacceptable behaviour required serious retribution in one form or another. One man, a continual pain-in-the-arse, was 'black-balled'. I don't mean that figuratively either, and in spite of constant showers it was some time before the boot polish finally faded.

All of this behaviour resulted from the more relaxed atmosphere and greater leisure time we now enjoyed which also allowed us freedom for various excursions. Devizes and Trowbridge were only a few miles away but the centre of Melksham was within walking distance. In the evenings at the cinema we would hope to see something displaying the charms of Betty Grable, Rita Hayworth, Vera-Ellen or, in particular, Jane Russell. We were at the age when chests were significant. There was an excellent fish and chip shop nearby. Following a visit to this, and the pub next door, we would amble back to camp, perhaps swinging round any convenient lamp-posts, and usually bellowing out an obscene ditty or two:

"We are from Green Street, good girls are we;

We take a pride in our virginity.
We take all precautions
Against all abortions
For we are the Green Street Girls.
Ra!
Ra! Ra!
Ra! Ra! Ra! Ra! Ra! Ra!
Our Flight Sergeant is a bloody fool;
He's only got a teeny-weeny tool.
It's alright for keyholes
And little girlies' wee-holes,
But we are the Green Street Girls.
Ra! ... etc."

Some miserable old man, no doubt resembling my present staid self, would usually open a window and suggest that we behaved ourselves. There was on camp the usual NAAFI offering chips and other culinary delights, drinks and leisure facilities, also a small 'Astra' cinema converted from one of the huts, but visiting them did not constitute 'an outing', which leaving the confines of the station did, not to mention the opportunities for meeting members of the opposite sex. There were a few civilian girls serving in the NAAFI and, however accommodating they might be, they were hardly enough to supply the demand.

On a number of weekends throughout that winter of 1951/2 the majority of us managed to go home, mostly on '48-hour passes' which were necessary to ensure that we weren't supposed to be on any sort of duty. After all, we were constantly reminded, we didn't have any time of our own, it all belonging to His Majesty, and leaves and passes were a concession, not a right. Railway Warrants could be applied for but were rationed to a certain number, which led to some unauthorised dealing. Those living relatively near to the camp might give, as their leave destination, the address of a colleague living hundreds of miles away, letting him use the warrant for a financial consideration cheaper than the full train fare. This would have had disastrous consequences if discovered by, say, an emergency call to report back for duty, which was most unlikely, or the vigilance of a member of the Transport Police. The great number of people in the services at that time, hardly any owning cars, meant that the railways, and the stations in particular, were always thronging with khaki, blue and navy uniforms. Any one of these service personnel could be stopped by the SPs to check the authenticity of his movements and the condition of his appearance.

I used all sorts of means of transport to get home and back in those short weekend breaks, firstly by train, which was a bit involved and expensive if you had used up your ration of warrants. London being a popular destination, a local coach company started running a regular service at reasonable cost, using a number of vehicles which the Commanding Officer permitted to line up on Friday evenings right inside the camp. These deposited you at a coach park at White City, from where I took a tube to central London and a Green Line bus home. For the return journey the coach left White City very late at night and arrived back at Melksham in the small hours. The only requirement was to be back in barracks and smart enough for the early parade. All the cross-country journeys I took during my service career were made before the introduction of the motorway network and I have recollections of waking from uncomfortable dozes at about three in the morning, freezing cold, and wiping the condensed breath from a window to ascertain our whereabouts.

"Newbury? Are you sure it's only Newbury?"

With a friend who came from my neck of the woods I tried hitch-hiking on one occasion. This practice was quite common in those days, motorists being more inclined to take pity on walkers, especially in uniform. We stood at the roadside outside the camp and tried to attract the attention of the passing cars, without success. Many of them were driven by RAF officers who had just emerged from the camp gates and we had to transform the thumbs-up hitch-hiking gesture into a salute in mid performance. Was what we were doing contrary to good service discipline? We weren't sure so we walked half a mile further along the road and tried again. Still no cars stopped, only, eventually, a lorry. This was going only about ten miles in our direction but we were getting desperate. We didn't seem to be enjoying the luck that others had experienced, or at least said they had, and when we got home, hours and hours later, we had walked a considerable part of the journey and climbed into about six assorted vehicles.

Soon I discovered that owners of motorcycles were permitted to keep their machines on camp, discretely parked in air-raid shelters behind the huts, so I thought it was about time I woke mine up and got it going again. It was a very old BSA 250cc bike, pre-war in fact, and had certainly never been driven by me as far as I was proposing to take it now. I donned my overcoat, gauntlets and goggles; no helmets in those days. Leaving home late at night I went across country through Marlow to pick up the Great West Road before Reading, then on through Newbury, Hungerford and Marlborough, turning off at Beckhampton crossroads towards Devizes and then Melksham. It was a dry night but it had rained earlier and about a third of the way into the journey I drove straight into a dip in the road full of water. The engine stalled and I put my feet down into a small lake about a foot deep. There was no point in going back home so, once I had persuaded the bike to start up again, I pressed on. All the way down, in what was now the early morning, I had the good fortune to meet no obstacles, red traffic lights or other reasons to take my feet off their rests. Unbeknown to me, the action of the cold slipstream on my wet trousers caused my legs to go dead. I coasted up to the camp gate, bristling with guards and Station Police, and put a leg out. It had no feeling or use and I fell onto the road in a heap with the machine on top of me! The next time I drove back to camp on it the weather was perfect but cold. It was so dry and clear that I dispensed with the cumbersome goggles. On arrival my mates stared at me and suggested that I look in the mirror. My eyeballs resembled red billiard balls.

Having my own transport not only facilitated home trips but widened the scope of local activities, allowing me to explore the countryside more freely and make off-duty trips into Bath. I was warned about the sudden hump-backed bridge on the road to Trowbridge. Not long before our arrival, an airman had come across this in the dark at too great a speed, taken off into the void and killed himself.

A number of motorcycle enthusiasts had formed them-selves into a club and were allowed to use an old hut as a headquarters and garage. One of these lads went all round the camp selling raffle tickets at a pound each, the prize being his motorcycle. He was shortly being posted away and reasoned that it was more convenient, and possibly more profitable, to dispose of it in that way. We all had a go and to his surprise it was won by someone in my hut.

"I know nothing about motorbikes," he confided to me, "and I certainly can't ride one. Would you come with me and have a look at it?"

We found it parked on its stand in the clubhouse, looking very good and apparently not very old. I wheeled it outside, kick-started it and drove it round the block.

"Well, you've got a bargain there!" I told him. "How are you going to get it home?"

"My brother could ride it. I'll get him to come down and take me home on the back of it."

The weeks went by and our own postings loomed.

"You'll have to get that bike of yours away very soon." I pointed out.

"I know. My brother won't come down and I don't know what to do."

I pondered. "Where do you live?" He mentioned somewhere in the Midlands.

"If your folks will give me a bed for the night and you pay my fare back I'll take you home on it."

"Thanks. That'll be a real weight off my shoulders."

The next weekend we went to the clubhouse to dig it out but where it had been parked there now stood just an empty frame on empty forks. The wheels had gone and so had the tank, the handlebars and many of the important components, such as the carburettor and the exhaust.

"Who's pinched all these bits?" we asked a member.

"Several of us. It stood here un-used and obviously abandoned so we took any bits we wanted."

So much for his prize! I wished that I had won it.

The arrangements for eating at Melksham were much on the same lines as we were used to, although the quality of the food and catering was somewhat better. As was standard throughout the service, every day the Orderly Officer on duty had to pass along the mess hall, accompanied by the Orderly Sergeant with notebook at the ready, stopping at every trestle table to ask, "Any complaints?" To which the only answer that would not get you into some sort of trouble was "No sir!"

To keep us up to scratch and to remind us that we were expected to maintain our equipment in good order, we were still obliged to undergo regular Kit Inspections. By now we had learned a few wrinkles, knowing exactly how things were to be laid out on the bed and the best and quickest ways of cleaning and polishing all the articles to be displayed. Surprisingly it was often possible to have an item missing but still get away without this being noticed. The inspecting party would always enter the building from the road end and work its way along the beds, sometimes clockwise and sometimes anti-clockwise. As soon as your lay-out had been approved you were permitted to dismantle it and pack your belongings away. If any of us were lacking, say, a pair of socks, we would arrange for the deficiency to occur at the far end of the room and behind officialdom's back a pair would be thrown across from someone who had already been inspected.

A large part of the evening before had to be devoted to the use of Blanco, boot polish and Brasso, and to the cleaning and pressing of clothes, although one man would lounge about on his bed reading a book while all this activity went on around him. On the morning of the inspection, all he had to do was make up his bed, with the blanket and sheet pack all square, open up his suitcase and remove from it a duplicate set of kit and clothing, all bulled-up and neatly folded, and lay it out. I have no idea how he acquired all this, although it was always a good idea to make a good friend of someone in Stores.

The loss of a piece of equipment did not normally result in being put on a charge. A clerical procedure would be invoked for obtaining a replacement, payment being deducted from your wages for two of the item in question. You paid for the one you lost and the one that replaced it! It was so much easier just to nick someone else's!

An occasional and unpopular event, wherever you were stationed, was the AOC's Inspection. This was an official visit by the Air Officer Commanding, a distinguished and daunting personage of 'Air' rank, much more important than the Station Commander, who was usually a Group Captain. Periodically he would make what amounted to a State Visit to each of the RAF stations under his command. The advent of this momentous occasion was the cause of more frenzied activity and 'bull' than we had seen before, especially to the barrack room and its surroundings,. The lino floor was buffed to perfection, the walls washed down, the windows cleaned, all furniture dusted and polished and paint applied to any areas needing attention. There were two stoves in the hut with flues rising to the apex of the roof. During the winter evenings we would sit with our feet up on these, sometimes burning the leather of our boots. These stoves had to be allowed to go out and cool down, then were completely emptied of all ash and cleaned inside then 'blacked' until they gleamed. The two large metal coal containers had to be emptied, cleaned and painted, black on the outside and white on the inside! The coals were then washed and carefully replaced. Outside the appearance of the camp suggested that the CO had authorised the purchase of all the white paint in the county. It adorned the edges of roads, any railings and countless stones laid neatly to form borders for pathways and entrances. The land in front of and between huts was scrupulously weeded and the areas of grass in front of most buildings trimmed down to resemble a billiard table, sometimes with the aid of nail-scissors.

"Will the AOC inspect all this lot, corporal?"

"Of course not. He'll go round on a short pre-determined route with the CO, turn up on parade and bunk off to the Officers' Mess. The simple fact of his visit makes all this effort necessary; he knows without seeing it that it will have been done. It provides a legitimate reason for the money to be spent on regular maintenance."

On the big day we rose early, assumed our 'best blue' uniforms, all freshly pressed and polished, gave the hut a final sweep and dust, 'fell in' outside and were marched onto the parade ground with the rest of the inmates. With the assistance of the band we drilled and lined up for inspection by the great man, resplendently adorned with much gold braid, and his entourage. The VIP party walked back and forth, pausing only momentarily for the AOC to pass a few words at random with an individual or two.

"Everything alright, aircraftman?"

"Yes sir, perfectly sir!"

"Good."

One of the other officers, a few paces behind, said to him "Well done, man; that's the only answer. What's your name?"

Now in answering this question you prefaced the reply with your rank, in this case Aircraftman, or 'AC', as in 'AC Smith'. But this particular airman's name was Bee.

"AC Bee, sir."

"ABC?"

"No sir, not ABC sir. AC Bee sir."

"What do you mean? You can't be ABC!"

"I'm not sir; I'm AC Bee," he replied, now sweating profusely. The officer turned to a senior NCO, armed with the customary notebook and pen. "See if you can find out what his name is; I'll go and talk to someone sensible."

The official party returned to the dais and we paraded past them in our various Flights to honour them with our best 'eyes right' and salute, and marched back to our quarters. After this, things could get back to normal and we re-lit the stoves. In that cold winter we used the coal at a faster rate than was allowed for by the regular deliveries so forays into the coal yard were made in the dead of night. This was a highly risky operation as the yard was, of course, out of bounds and penalties for discovery severe. We were, in effect, stealing.

Time came round for the regular FFI inspection of our intimate parts and we 'stood by our beds' ready to drop our trousers and pants as the Medical Officer approached. It turned out to be a young woman! I don't know who was most embarrassed, the inspector or the inspected, but with a hint of pinkness about her features she completed the task, one chap remarking, "I wonder which of us will be the first to display visible interest in her as a woman?"

Wages were paid, here as throughout the service, by means of a fortnightly Pay Parade. This took place in a large empty hangar, in front of which stood a fast-dilapidating wartime Lancaster bomber. Hundreds of us marched in and stood to attention until our name was called.

"Clinton, R."

"Sir, 503!"

You stepped smartly forward and halted. A clerk read out the appropriate amount from a ledger, incorporating any stoppages imposed and any deductions for family allowances you had authorised, and the officer in charge counted out the money from his cash box and laid it on the table. You performed the ungainly operation of simultaneously scooping up the cash, saluting, stepping back a pace and about-turning, and returned to your place. The paying officer had signed for the substantial amount of money involved and had the task of counting out these hundreds of payments, any discrepancies at the end being his responsibility. At least that is what we understood.

As I have said, general discipline was not as severe as on square-bashing but there was one individual to be feared and that was the Station Warrant Officer who was responsible for all policing and general order around the camp. This particular SWO was strict about appearance, including his own. He marched about with erect and precise bearing, immaculately dressed. Needless to say his hair conformed to regulations but on the rare occasions when he was seen bare headed it was apparent that he possessed a magnificent shock of red hair, of which he was very proud. One of his less endearing habits was to stop an airman about the camp, tell him to get his hair cut and report back, then consider the result unsatisfactory and order him back for another trim.

The following incident was related to me by a usually reliable mate. The barber, a civilian, asked one man on his second visit in two days, "Who is doing this to you?"

"The SWO," came the reply.

"Yes, well he'll soon be wanting a haircut himself..."

When he did, he was given a shorter cut than anyone had ever seen at that time. All his glorious locks fell to the floor and he was nearly bald. He rose from the chair and examined the result in a mirror. Thinking fast, he said to the barber, and for the benefit of the airmen waiting their turn in the chair, "That's the best haircut I've had in years," and tipped the hairdresser handsomely.

Sooner or later everybody would have to serve a spell on guard duty throughout the evening and night, on a shift basis. I manned a small hut near the main entrance, the duties consisting mainly of checking the permanent passes of anyone leaving and the credentials of anyone entering, and saluting smartly anyone entitled to be so honoured.

There was a stove in the hut which I dutifully kept supplied with coal but somehow I achieved the impossible and made it go out, incurring the wrath of the Station Police in the guardroom and my relief guard. Another evening I manned a similar position adjacent to the rear entrance. The camp stood between two roads that eventually converged on Melksham and the back gate was the shortest route to and from town for pedestrians. The small post was a long way from the residential huts, and indeed from anything at all, there being no guardroom at that gate. A very tall lamppost threw a circle of bright light over the whole area to enable passes and identity cards to be checked. After a rush of airmen returning from an evening out it went very quiet and was boring work. Curiously I wondered what controlled the overhead lamp and discovered a large switch on the end of the shack, which I flicked off and on quickly to check, whereupon the lamp went out and stayed out, leaving me and the surroundings in complete darkness. Further switching produced no effect. There was a telephone in the guard post connected to the main guardroom for use in extreme emergency but I hesitated from using it for fear of the consequences, particularly if the problem could be attributed to an action on my part. After I had agonised for about ten minutes the light came on again, slowly. It was one of those gas-filled lamps that require a warming-up period which I had not realised; and me nearly an electrician!

One day, early in February, our WRAF officer English teacher was particularly late in class and we indulged in the usual schoolboy behaviour with chalk and rulers and bawdy singing. Eventually she arrived and we stood to attention.

"Please sit down" she gasped and, throwing herself into her chair, she collapsed over the desk, sobbing uncontrollably. A long pause ensued. Then someone said "Is anything the matter, ma'am?" but received no immediate reply. Eventually she sat up and collected herself.

"Haven't you heard?"

"Heard what, ma'am?"

"The King is dead!" And she burst into tears again.

We were at a loss.

"That's very sad, ma'am. Did you know him personally?"

"No, of course not. But you don't understand. I hold a commission in his name. I have sworn an oath of allegiance to THAT MAN!" So had all of us, as it happened, or his heirs and successors of course, but she collapsed again and we never did get an English lesson that day. With immediate effect all commissioned ranks had to wear a wide black armband throughout the period of official mourning. The gullible one in our hut was easily persuaded that other ranks had to turn their cap-badges upside down. It was some time before an eagle-eyed NCO spotted this. Overnight, King's Regulations became Queen's Regulations and we were now all 'New Elizabethans'.

The day finally arrived for our Trade Examination, passing it being necessary to go forth in the world to a proper posting as a qualified tradesman. It was an event approached with some trepidation. We needn't have worried however, as the whole thing was very simple, it being obvious that pains were taken to see that no-one ever failed. The 'practical', for example, was laughable. We were taken individually into an examination room laid out with various pieces of apparatus and conducted round by a genial sergeant.

"Now lad, this item here... I don't have to tell you it's a squirrel cage motor, do I?"

"No sergeant."

"No, I thought not. What is this then?"

"A Kent Clear Screen system," we both said in unison.

"You do know how to service it, don't you?"

"Yes sergeant."

"Splendid. Now, in a battery charging room, what is the correct dilution percentage of sulphuric acid for a working solution?"

Oh crikey! I couldn't remember, but inspiration struck.

"I would, of course, refer to Poster 20, which, by Queen's Regulations, has to be displayed in all charging rooms."

"I can hardly fail you with that answer," he said.

The result of this 'searching' examination was that, in common with all my colleagues, I was now a qualified Electrical Mechanic Ground, raised in rank to AC1 or Aircraftman First Class, still only just off the lowest status possible.

With a fellow hut-mate, a lad called Mo, I was given my 'permanent' posting, to a place called Harpur Hill which, I learned, was near to Buxton in Derbyshire. Postings were decided arbitrarily by clerks at a central administration centre somewhere. There were always rumours that destinations could be 'wangled' but in practice the most common outcome was to be posted hundreds of miles from home. There was, for instance, a large Royal Air Force station at Bovingdon, a mere three miles from my home address, and I couldn't see any reason why I could not have spent the rest of my service career there.

We were given our railway warrants and started our booking-out procedure, a farce carried out on leaving camp, wherever you were stationed. Bedding had to be returned to Stores and a series of signatures had to be obtained on a list. The Medical Officer signed that you were fit, Stores that you had returned everything and even the padre, for some unknown reason; nicking hymn books perhaps? So on down the list, ending with the Station Warrant Officer, to confirm that you had got all the other autographs and discharged any punishments, before returning the form to the Squadron Office. The various officials could get a good bit of fun out of all this. They might each insist that they could not sign until a certain other signature had been obtained and it was not uncommon to spend a whole morning going round in circles until the form was completed.

After a fairly interesting and informative sixteen weeks we put on our 'best blue', packed everything else in our kitbags and set out for our new destinations, looking forward to utilising our new skills in a rewarding qualified occupation.

How naïve we were!

4. RAF Harpur Hill

Mo and I arrived at Buxton railway station, after a somewhat involved cross-country journey, late on a February evening. There was a group of local characters standing at a bus stop.

"Excuse me, do you know if the RAF at Harpur Hill normally send some transport for new arrivals?"

"Shouldn't think so; we've never seen any. Hop on this bus; it goes up that way."

We clambered aboard, squeezing our kit-bags down the aisle and the vehicle chugged off over the hill that leads out of town, then slowly up the steeper side-road to the south and through the village of Harpur Hill, where we were shown where to alight, right by the camp. There was no gate or entrance as such, just a few modern-looking buildings. One was a NAAFI and another was obviously living quarters, with the ground floor corner room acting as a basic sort of guard-room. We attracted the attention of a passing airman and he took us into this room.

"New arrivals, eh?"

"Yes. This looks a posh place."

"Oh it is. We each have an individual room to our self with all modern comforts, just like a hotel. Unfortunately you won't be living here though, you'll be in the 'top camp.'"

"Who lives here, then?"

"You graduate to it. As men get demobbed or posted, the vacancies are filled from the other part of the camp in rotation, if you live that long."

As it turned out, I stayed at that location for only six months and never did get to live in the modern part.

"Hang on, I'll phone for your transport."

A lorry arrived and conveyed us back through the village, left into a rough track and, after more climbing, eventually passed through an open and unattended gate and deposited us outside a wooden hut which was the Transit Billet. A bored airman unlocked his store cupboard and handed us bed linen and blankets, for which we had to sign and then claim a bed.

In the morning we had a surprise. We had travelled the previous day in pleasant, sunny, spring-like conditions and arrived on a fine evening but the view from the window now showed a considerable layer of snow across the countryside, which was mostly fields and dry stone walls. The Transit Billet Orderly explained.

"That's quite common. One winter it was so bad that the camp was completely isolated and everybody got an unexpected extended leave. We are on the edge of the Peak District, you know. This is supposed to be the highest RAF station in the country. And the smallest. There are only about three hundred personnel."

'And the scruffiest,' we might have added later, when we got to know it. We returned our bed clothes and made our way to the headquarters building for instructions, crossing a piece of roughly tarmac-covered waste ground with plenty of gravel on it.

"Stand still those men!" We stood still. A Flight Sergeant approached us and lectured us about the evils of desecrating the hallowed surface of a parade ground.

"*This* is the parade ground?"

"Yes."

"Well we only arrived last night. It doesn't look like a parade ground, does it, Flight?"

He permitted himself a slight smile. "I suppose not. But you'll know next time, won't you? Carry on!"

At Headquarters we were advised which hut we were to call home. There were about six of them, standing forlornly on a sloping piece of ground. Inside they lacked that tender loving care that had been lavished on our previous lodgings. Not exactly dirty, they were, in fact, swept through each morning and the bed spaces made reasonably tidy, but they were somewhat primitive. There was no nice weather-proof corridor to the ablutions, the washing and bathing facilities being in a separate block some yards away. Dashing across, partly-dressed, on a sharp, windy and possibly wet morning was exhilarating! The water wasn't always hot either.

Having claimed two obviously unoccupied beds and deposited our belongings we returned, as ordered, to the Headquarters block to meet the Commanding Officer. A camp of this size could only run to a Wing Commander, not the usual Group Captain, and in view of the small number of new arrivals he liked to greet them personally.

Now I have always believed that the next piece of nonsense was an evil scheme thought up by the CO and his sergeant to amuse themselves.

"Now then," said the sergeant, "I shall say 'Attention' then open the CO's door, march in and report 'two new arrivals, sir'. I shall give you a 'quick march, right wheel' in very rapid succession. The reason for this is it is only a small office and if you take more than a few paces in before turning in front of his desk you will find yourselves behind him. You will then halt, do a left turn and salute."

We did as instructed. The floor had been polished to resemble a skating rink and we were wearing our boots with their well-worn metal studs. The sudden right turn had no effect at all on our momentum so we slid straight on, careering into the back wall and collapsing in a heap on the floor. Without any change of expression the CO asked us about our training, gave a brief explanation of our working role and dismissed the two of us to seek out our place of employment. This turned out to be a modest-sized building with a few work benches in it and a small number of airmen lounging about in armchairs. A Senior Aircraftman climbed to his feet and introduced himself.

"Is this the Electrical Workshop?" we asked. He laughed.

"It's the everything workshop for the whole camp. We've got a blacksmith, a sheet-metal worker, a carpenter, an engineer, some we're not sure about and, since your arrival, three electricians."

"We're looking forward to doing our share of the work in our trade at last." He laughed again.

"How long have you signed on for?" he asked us.

"Four years."

"Well there's something about the next three and a half years you need to know and that is that you'll be lucky if you do any work in your trade at all. Has it not occurred to you that Melksham is churning out hundreds of electricians a week, regardless of their necessity, because with all the vast numbers of recruits something has to done with them? The same goes, of course, for all the other trades."

"There must be a few jobs, mustn't there? Camp maintenance and that sort of thing?"

"For some time I've been the only electrician here, dealing with all the very occasional jobs that come along. Now some idiot has decreed that there should be three of us but remember, I am the SAC and therefore your superior, so I do any electrical jobs that occasionally crop up."

So we became accustomed to a life of boredom. Each day we would sit with our feet up on a large stove in the centre of the workshop and read the morning papers. Then we would swap them round and read some more, finally screwing them up into a ball and playing soccer with it between the benches. A bit of sadistic fun could be had by wrapping newspaper round a heavy metal block, and shaping it to appear spherical, while the victim was elsewhere relieving himself. On his return he would be challenged to 'score a goal from there'.

We fought mock battles from behind the benches, heaving chairs and stools across the room at each other. On one occasion I stood up from behind my bench a little too quickly and caught the leg of a flying wooden chair right over one eye. It bled profusely and I went along to the small medical centre.

"I am not reporting sick," I told the orderly emphatically, knowing the implications of that action. It involved returning all kit to stores, including the clothes you were not wearing and reporting to the Medical Officer with your small pack containing pyjamas and toiletries on the assumption that hospitalisation might result. The arrangement was, of course, intended to daunt all but the genuinely ill and to deter malingerers. I just wanted a piece of sticking plaster. My protestations that I had not been involved in the serious matter of fisticuffs were treated with some suspicion, even though I invented a non-existent doorpost. It's still possible to see my little 'war wound' over one eyebrow.

Very occasionally the officer with responsibility for the workshop put in a token appearance. Hastily we would grab a piece of wood or metal and be 'working' on it. He wasn't deceived, of course, as he understood the situation, but honour would be satisfied.

During the colder weather, some entertainment could be had by lighting the stove, which was very old and very reluctant to get going. We would fill it with scraps of wood and cardboard, topped off with some coke and then pour in sump oil or other flammable liquids. Having drawn the short straw someone would approach it with a lighted taper while the others retreated to a safe distance, for there were several possible outcomes. Often it would just not light while at other times it would ignite with an explosion. On at least one occasion it blew up, the separate layers of its cast iron body parting company and parts of the tall chimney pipe distributing themselves to far corners of the shop.

Some of us worked at times on personal projects to pass the hours away. I produced, slowly, a fancy rear light assembly for my motorcycle from a piece of aluminium. There was only about one official job that I worked on towards the end of my time at Harpur Hill and that was, I suspect, spurious. The officer claimed to have thought up an idea for a gadget to record by means of electric lamps the answers given in a services quiz. Mo and I were set to knock it up out of plywood and then solder all the numerous internal connections. However slowly we worked, its progress was never monitored and it was still only partly made on the day we moved away to our next postings.

A most welcome interruption to our uninteresting life was the visit, twice daily, of the NAAFI van, the NAAFI canteen being too far away for short breaks. A pleasant mature lady dispensed tea, sticky buns and cheerful conversation and helped to break the monotony for as long as we could manage to stretch the visit out. In the evening, trips would be made to the canteen itself, the shortest route being by a footpath across the top of a small mountain to the road and then through the village. Although it was the better half of the year it was sometimes raining and nearly always blowing a cold gale on the highest and most exposed part of the journey. At the NAAFI we had more chips, a glass of beer and the chance to hand over coupons to buy sweets (at this time confectionery was still 'on the ration').

It did not take long to get to know the camp, or at least the parts open to us, but just past the workshop high and very secure fencing marked the boundary of the Danger Area, entry to which required special authorisation. This was where the real work took place, for the station was a unit for the storage and maintenance of bombs and explosive devices. The men working with them were armourers and, because of the nature of their work, their uniforms were invariably dirty and worn. This was accepted by all and was, no doubt, why the rest of us were not challenged too severely over our appearance.

The Danger Area was normally 'out of bounds' other than for armoury personnel and I found myself inside it on only two occasions. At the entrance was a substantial guardroom at which your authority for entry had to be proved, your identity verified and all items that might ignite a flame such as matches and lighters removed from your pockets. Hidden underground were several levels of large tunnels where work was carried out. I cannot recall why I had to go down the lift into this underworld; possibly a rare electrical job had arisen.

On the other occasion I was detailed for guard duty at an entrance at the far end of the Danger Area. The way of getting to it was by train! The extent of this open countryside was considerable and although the camp may have been small in terms of personnel, in area it must have ranked among the largest. Across this tract of hilly terrain a narrow-gauge railway ran, for the purpose of deliveries to and from a series of bunkers spread, for safety, at well-spaced distances from each other. Having drawn a rifle and a few live rounds I was obliged to stand on the rear ledge of a small diesel locomotive and travel to the end of the line, a short distance from a guard hut alongside a break in the fence that was filled with a five-barred gate bristling with barbed wire. It seemed miles from anywhere. The man I was relieving ran past me and jumped onto the engine.

"I'll be back at the end of your shift," the driver called out, and disappeared into the distance, leaving me in complete isolation. I took up my position, occasionally breaking the tedium by sloping arms and marching about. My only instructions had been not to let anyone into this sensitive enclosure under any circumstances.

After a while I noticed a man yanking open the gate.

"Halt, who goes there?" I demanded, in true sentry-like manner. He laughed and started ushering sheep through the gap into the confines of the camp.

"You're not supposed to come in here, are you?"

"I'd better be; all this is my grazing land."

In the little hut there was a field telephone. I had no idea to whom it was connected but I wound its handle anyway. No-one answered. Having deposited a whole flock of sheep inside the fence the farmer pulled the gate closed and departed. Naturally I was somewhat apprehensive until, in due course, I had quietly consulted a mate who confirmed that this was a regular occurrence.

Again I explored different methods of travelling to and from home on a number of 'forty-eights'. By rail the journey from home was up to Euston, a stroll along to St Pancras and thence northwards through Derby, which could always be identified in the dark by the distinctive smell of a steam-railway town. Changing at Miller's Dale took us onto the most attractive scenic branch line through tunnels and over high bridges to Buxton. With a companion I had one more and final attempt at hitch-hiking, with no great success. The first vehicle that responded to our gesticulations was going to Peterborough. Neither of us knew where that was and the driver had no idea where it was situated in relation to our destinations, so we went there. It was substantially off the direct route and hours were wasted in assorted cars and vans and on foot, getting home.

It was obviously time to dig out the old 'Beezer', check it over and top up the tank. The distance, on the old roads, was the best part of 150 miles. The A6 passed through both St Albans, near home, and Buxton, so it seemed logical to get onto that road and stay on it. Suitably attired, I set off through Luton, Bedford, Kettering, Leicester, Loughborough and to Derby. Beyond that the road started entering the craggy valleys of the Peak District with an increasing number of sharp bends. One hairpin doubled back on itself so severely that I shot across the wrong side of the road, to the consternation of both myself and the oncoming driver. It was not long before I discovered that the quickest route for the final forty miles from Derby was over high and relatively straight roads via Ashbourne.

Excursions were now possible and with a companion on the pillion I saw something of the spectacular countryside, such as the Snake Pass, the Ladybower Reservoir, Dove Valley and the wild road past the Cat and the Fiddle, 'the highest inn in the country'. I acquired a basic camera to record some of these outings. It was an 'Ensign Ful-Vue' box camera which took square pictures on size 120 roll film. There were no refinements such as focussing or speed adjustment and a small choice of alternative apertures, but it had a surprisingly good lens and a very useful large viewfinder. It also had 'flash' sockets and could have a flashgun attached to it using disposable one-off miniature flash bulbs. On my home visits I would disappear into the cupboard under the stairs with a few basic chemicals and dishes and produce contact prints.

One of my new friends persuaded me, one weekend, to take him on the bike to his home in Sheffield. That was very pleasant; he had a stunning girlfriend and his mother said to me "Ee, yer do talk nice". My Hertfordshire origins show clearly in my voice as, no doubt, all southerners were one to her. The journey home in late evening was eventful but somewhere near Taddington, with some seven or eight miles still to go, the rear tyre developed a puncture so we walked the rest of the way, one of us alternately trudging beside the machine, which was ticking over in first gear. We deposited it in the forecourt of the garage in Harpur Hill for repair later, climbed over the hill to our billet and collapsed into bed sometime during the night.

On one of my return journeys from leave I took back to camp a mate from St Albans. Well into the journey I felt him nestle closer to me on the pillion. It was only when I spoke to him later on that I realised he was fast asleep and that a sudden acceleration would have shot him off the back. We had with us a small suitcase, tied onto a pannier. Somewhere beyond Derby it fell off, the string disappearing into the night. A lonely cottager in his pyjamas stared goggle-eyed at our request for a length of stout string. Well... it was three o'clock in the morning!

The local centre of civilisation was Buxton. Sometimes we took the bus but as often as not we walked the two miles down into town to sample the pubs, the cinema, the chip shop and the local talent. One night in the cinema the second-feature film proved an unexpected delight. It was a documentary about my home town! Hemel Hempstead was just embarking on its metamorphosis into a satellite New Town and to encourage Londoners to make the move to the countryside the delights of the place were illustrated in a public-service film 'A Home of Your Own'. It was an experience, in deepest Derbyshire, to watch the people travelling through the roads and lanes of my native haunts, and setting off in quite the wrong directions for their apparent destinations! It was very nice at times to take advantage of a generous concession by the proprietor of the Spa Hotel who made his excellent indoor swimming pool available free of charge to Air Force personnel.

One evening, against my better nature, I went into town with several others for a double celebration. One man was to be demobbed shortly and one married. The occasion was merely an excuse for an evening of hard drinking as became evident when the self-appointed leader of the party got the landlord to fill the largest jug on the premises and to top it up at frequent intervals. Silly games were played, all involving swallowing more beer in various eccentric ways, and all with the forfeit for failure of having to drink another pint without pausing. I managed to stay sober but the penalty at closing time was finding myself in the role of chaperone to a bunch of inebriates. On the way out of town they had to be persuaded down from lampposts and out of gardens and side alleys, from where they emerged triumphantly bearing dustbin lids. They discovered that spun through the air upside-down like a Frisbee these could travel some distance. Out of town they would as often be lurching about in fields as on the road and it was with some relief that we reached camp. Then, of course, they mostly got into the wrong huts and tried to get into occupied beds, so had I not gone with them I would still, like everyone else, have been thoroughly disturbed after getting to sleep for the night. My bed space was the one nearest the door so every evening after general agreement I had to get out of bed to switch the light out. There invariably followed a succession of late-comers putting it on again and leaving it on as they fell into their 'pits'. I soon fixed a length of string from the switch, up over a rafter to the head of my bed.

Many evenings, naturally, were spent in the billet although entertainment was virtually non-existent. On one return from home I managed somehow to take a small portable gramophone with me in a shoulder bag and we played a handful of records until they wore out. One song, a hit at the time, went: "My heart sighs for you; Cries for you; Dies for you,"– which always prompted one chap, who we called 'Gloria', to climb onto a table, wrap a towel round himself as a skirt, flutter his long eyelashes and sing along, falsetto. He looked rather like Melvyn Hayes; he couldn't have been, could he?

There is a universal service maxim 'never volunteer' – on the grounds that you will always let yourself in for more and worse than you expected. But when an opportunity came to spend a week down at Bisley in Surrey, helping at the shooting competitions, to break the monotony I put my name down and went. It turned out to be an interesting and far from onerous experience, which could be preceded and followed by weekends at home. The numerous rifle ranges, spread over many square miles of open country, varied from short distance to those with targets one thousand yards away. The competitors embraced marksmen from all walks of life, both civilian and various branches of the services. They weren't worked for long hours and nor were we helpers. Everybody turned out at a decent hour in the morning for one firing session and again after lunch, finishing not too late in the afternoon. The job for us 'erks' was in the butts, in trenches set below the line of fire underneath the targets which were mounted on large square boards on pulleys like a sash window but counter-weighted with a similar board for indicating the score. After each burst of fire over our heads we would record the results on the score board and haul it up in place of the target, which we would prepare for the next competitor by pasting pieces of paper over the bullet holes. Up again it would go, and so on. The competitors scanned the scores through telescopes.

Apart from these working periods, the large numbers of volunteers were not greatly supervised or monitored. We slept in circular bell tents, six of us with our feet towards the pole, each on a 'safari bed', a contraption put together from a kit of canvas sheeting and several lengths of metal rod. The two disadvantages of this piece of field kit were that as it stood only an inch or two high anyone over a certain weight pressed it down and may as well have been sleeping on the ground, and the supporting legs touched the surface away from the edges so that movement away from the centre of gravity shot you out of bed. With the sessions finishing so early in the afternoon I even managed to get home in the middle of the week as well as before and after.

Upon my return to Harpur Hill I soon found that I had been detailed for duty as Transit Billet Orderly. On the face of it this was another cushy job, involving no more than living in the billet for a period and distributing and re-claiming bedding as required by transient personnel. The snag was the amount of this bedding that for a period was your responsibility which – incorporating sheets, blankets and pillows – ran into large quantities. Having signed for all this, there was a remote but real possibility of some officious officer demanding an inventory, the cost of any discrepancies being charged to the incumbent orderly as well as any disci-plinary action. Such a case had occurred within the memory of some of my fellows. In an ideal world you wouldn't sign for anything you hadn't counted but this would have taken a very long time and in practice the orderly you were relieving would not be prepared to wait for such a check, even though it was widely believed that the quantities of various items had mysteriously decreased over a period.

"Bugger that! Sign here. I'm off!" Like everyone else I had to hope that no disaster would befall. It didn't, and I had in similar fashion to get authority for the stock passed to the next orderly without question.

Inevitably there was a 'village idiot' in our midst who be-came the butt of practical jokes and minor forms of torture for some misdemeanour, real or invented. On one occasion, for some petty reason, this unfortunate individual, while wearing pyjamas, had his wrists and ankles tethered and was carried across the camp road to the opposite side, with fire-crackers attached to his feet. The perpetrators laughed at his attempts to get back by shuffling his legs backwards and forwards while scraping holes in the seat of his pyjama trousers on the rough gravel, especially when a lorry approached and he had to speed up his jerky efforts. I never participated in these disgraceful practices nor, I regret, did I attempt to stop them although any protest would have fallen on deaf ears. As I have said, communal life is not everybody's cup of tea.

The Airmen's Mess was at the top camp, convenient for the residents there and not too bad for the others at most times who, certainly on working days, were passing that way. The food varied from alright to not very good and all of it unim-aginative. As usual, the view through the hatches of the kitchen together with its smell did nothing to titillate the taste buds. The fish one day gave off a most suspicious aroma and was largely left untouched. Along came the Orderly Officer on his rounds.

"Any complaints?"

"Yes sir; the fish is off!"

The young officer raised his eyebrows and the Orderly Sergeant nearly fainted away on the spot. The officer lifted a plate and sniffed at it, pulling a face.

"By Jove I think you're right. Sergeant, get something done."

"Yes sir." said the sergeant, taking the name and number of the brave complainant. Several days later we saw this daring young man. He was marching about in full bulled-up kit and obviously on 'jankers'.

"What are you on a charge for?"

"Making a frivolous complaint."

"How did you do that?"

"It was that bloody piece of fish. It ended up being inspected by the Medical Officer who declared it fit for human consumption. That made me out of order in complaining. I protested that the Orderly Officer's opinion ought to be taken into account but all that happened was that I got three days' 'jankers'".

The food generally was really sub-standard and we wished that some way could be found to bring this to someone's attention. The opportunity presented itself before very long during an AOC's Inspection. As to be expected, this event led to a flurry of activity, some improvement to the appearance of our surroundings and the assembly on parade of the entire company for once dressed immaculately. A small contingent was selected as a Guard of Honour.

"Tell you what," said one of them, "if the jolly old AOC talks to me I shall tell him about the food."

"Bet you don't."

"Bet I do then."

On the day the Air Officer stopped in front of this very man and addressed him.

"Everything alright, airman?"

There was a short pause while we hoped for the best.

"No sir!"

"No? What do you mean, 'No'?"

"The food, sir; it's unpalatable."

"Good; good," said the AOC without hesitating. "I'm glad things are still the same as they were in my young days!" And he passed down the line. I had a feeling that more 'jankers' would ensue and, of course, nothing was done to improve the catering.

There was a bizarre event over the Easter weekend that theoretically placed virtually the whole camp on a charge. A notice was displayed granting leave for the Bank Holidays. It was worded ambiguously but after discussion we concluded that we were effectively on leave from Good Friday to Easter Monday inclusive. On our return we were surprised to learn that we should not have been missing on the intervening Saturday (!) and that consequently we were, theoretically, all charged with being Absent Without Leave, a serious offence. In practical terms, let alone the injustice, the whole three hundred of us could not be paraded before the CO, nor be subjected to communal punishment. No charge ever appeared on our documents and the whole silly matter was conveniently dropped.

Apart from such distractions, working life continued its wearisome way. In September 1952 the people who control these things decided in their mysterious way that it was about time I moved on somewhere else and I received my next posting.

From the smallest camp in the UK I was to go to the largest, St Athan in South Wales, hopefully to be able to make more use of my training.

I was wrong again.

5. RAF St Athan

RAF St Athan (without the superfluous 's' usually added) was much more the sort of place you might expect an RAF camp to be. It was some twelve miles or so west of Cardiff, on a branch line that weaved its way through Dinas Powys (which we never pronounced correctly according to the natives) and Barry, on through Bridgend and points west. I had instructions not to alight at St Athan but at the next station, more convenient for the Maintenance Unit to which I had been posted, which bordered on a flying unit. There was also, at this site, a substantial Royal Air Force hospital, plus a centre for 'boy-entrants' and other units. The complex was so large it was possible to take a local bus from one part to another.

The several entrances to the Maintenance Unit were merely unguarded side roads off the highway, the guardroom being situated among the central cluster of buildings. A large community of men with wives and families was accommodated in several streets of 'married quarters', which were proper houses so that civilians involved were not obliged to have their movements impeded by a main gate with guards. Set around the parade ground, a proper one, were various substantial brick buildings. Block 8, my new home, was one of a number of identical barrack blocks. These dormitories, on three floors, were spacious and comfortable and with central heating! A wing on each storey contained the ablution facilities. One block, the 'waffery', was exclusively for the WRAF contingent, under the eye of a strict sergeant who guarded her girls like a mother hen. Needless to say, this was 'out of bounds' for the boys. Other blocks included the Officers' and Sergeants' messes for both catering and social activities, the Headquarters, a large Astra Cinema, a NAAFI with canteen, games rooms and television lounge showing on a large screen programmes from the recently opened Welsh transmitter at Wenvoe, a church, an education centre and medical facilities. The Airmen's Mess, purely for eating in, was attractively decorated with a series of murals in cartoon format showing 'erks' suffering various pitfalls and embarrassments of service life. The food was a great improvement over that at my previous postings. Presumably all Catering Officers were given similar budgets and general guidelines but the variety of quality from one place to another was extraordinary. In spite of the undoubted difficulties of bulk preparation, some establishments, with a bit of imagination and pride in results, turned out a variety of quite desirable meals. Others are best forgotten.

Further away were the long rows of large workshops where our working days were spent, and I looked forward to having something to do, not so much out of a sense of duty and dedication as to occupy the otherwise seemingly endless days of boredom. Again I was, in the main, disappointed. There was little to do and, worse, we were under the authority of a Squadron Leader who demanded an apparent air of activity. I was one of a number of mechanics, some twenty or so, each allocated a bench and a stool in a large workshop dedicated to matters electrical. Very occasionally a proper job would come along; for example on one occasion a batch of metal boxes had to be fitted out with components and wired up throughout according to a diagram, and by working slowly we made this last a bit. Otherwise we would have a few bits of equipment on the bench and tinker with them for the benefit of anyone who might drop in. In the event of a VIP such as the AOC being in the vicinity we would be given a motor or something similar to 'service', which meant taking it apart slowly and reassembling it as many times as necessary.

The workshops were quite close to the adjacent flying unit, equipped with Gloster Meteors and daily we heard the unfamiliar sound of early jet engines running up to test speed.

The NAAFI breaks morning and afternoon offered welcome interruption, as did periodic visits to a drinking fountain on the wall outside.

"I wonder why it is, AC Clinton, that every time I pass by, you are having a drink," commented the Squadron Leader. Tempted to reply, "That's funny, sir, because every time I am having a drink you seem to pass by!" or "If I was properly occupied I wouldn't be". Instead I saluted and grinned sheepishly. In fact, the officer may well have been as frustrated as we were with the uninteresting life he was now leading, as we were given to understand that he had once been one of Guy Gibson's Dam Busters.

Now and then an opportunity arose on official business to visit some of the other workshops in which operations such as welding, painting or metalwork took place. Once we had some metal that had to be prepared for painting by being submerged in a large vat of trichloroethylene, which stripped off all grease and dirt and would, apparently, have taken off any fingers, for which reason we were always warned to stand well back.

Underneath the workshop's elevated office, from which the officer in charge surveyed his small empire, was a storeroom presided over by a WRAF. Her presence should have inhibited our colourful language but we soon found that it didn't bother her, or perhaps she just didn't understand it! It was generally assumed among the men that girls who joined the Air Force, which they weren't obliged to do, did so for one of two reasons; either they were escaping from an unfortunate relationship with a man or they were sex-starved and on the look-out for one. That certainly wasn't the case with this one, who was shy, very young but looked even younger and was somewhat plain. Up to that point, most of us had had little communication with the opposite sex within camp precincts and, as one chap put it, with typical male chauvinism, "Oh well, she's probably alright to practise on."

Our benches were supplied with compressed air for the operation of hand tools and we were warned strictly about the dangers of its use and consequences of any horse-play, the tale being related of the airman who had died as a result of an airline being inserted into his back passage.

Fortunately there were a number of leisure facilities provided so at least some of the off-duty hours could be spent usefully. In a block behind the mess, a number of rooms had been set aside for various clubs, such as model-making, motorcycling and so on. Having dabbled a bit in photography, I joined the Camera Club and invested in a better camera, which I bought off an acquaintance. It was a folding bellows type 120 size camera with a pathetic viewfinder (of the Box Brownie type) and without any built-in means of gauging exposure (so I purchased a light meter) but it had various shutter speeds and a stoppable iris. Focussing also had to be set by guesswork or the use of a separate rangefinder.

With this I snapped the local vicinity and the camp and developed the results in the Camera Club headquarters. This consisted of a room in which members could store their equipment and chemicals in separate lockers and a larger room for processing. In this were three darkrooms each equipped with a decent enlarger. Also provided were sinks, a print washer and a large mechanical drying and glazing machine. One of the members was a cook in the airmen's mess and it was a good idea to avoid being next after him in a sealed darkroom at the end of his shift. You could tell which one he had used by the distinctive cookhouse smell, consisting largely of onion with a touch of dirty washing-up water.

Those who seemed to enjoy the best life in the Air Force were the sports enthusiasts, who were consequently somewhat unpopular with those following less energetic pursuits. Sport was considered highly important and those engaged in it were often granted privileges such as the avoidance of special responsibilities like guard duty and, in the cases of particular talent, were sometimes even posted to a camp to join an elite to train in their speciality.

We were all supposed to participate in some game or other on one Sports Afternoon a week whether or not we had any inclination or ability. One of the Camera Club members, with his tongue firmly in his cheek, asked whether our interest could be classed as a sports activity for this purpose. Rather to our surprise this was granted and each Sports Afternoon saw us on parade ready to set off on an official Photographic Ramble instead of getting into shorts to pretend to play silly games.

In order to ensure that we were bona fide a sergeant inspected our cameras to see that they actually contained film, by observing a number through the little red window. It was an easy matter to slip a piece of newspaper behind this showing a figure of some sort, as some of us had no film and never took any photographs. Fortunately, no-one asked to see the finished results of our photography. Thirty-five millimetre or 'miniature' cameras, as they were usually called, had been around for some time but were by no means common. The few some of us had were a great mystery to the suspicious sergeant who couldn't understand why he was unable to see any film through a small window!

What we did, usually, was ramble down through Llantwit Major village to the beach, play about for a bit, lie around enjoying our unexpected leisure and amble back, stopping at the little café run by the wife of one of the officers (who wouldn't split on her customers).

The camp's Astra Cinema screened all the latest releases but the best centre of entertainment, not too far away on the train, was Cardiff. The first sight outside the station was a row of tired-looking old tarts, whose layers of cosmetics failed to conceal their haggard appearance.

"I wouldn't touch them with yours, let alone mine," a mate commented.

The first time I went to the capital of the Principality and to the cinema I disgraced myself. At the end everybody rose and I marched out, wondering why I was the only one to leave. The locals glared at me; they were, of course, standing for the Welsh National Anthem.

At the theatre I saw a number of variety shows, most memorably one starring Max Wall. His Professor Wallofski sketch, which he was obliged by request to go on performing for many years, was new to me. The funny walk, the falling through a chair and the arms that could be extended to reach the piano all had me in tears of laughter. Another time I made the mistake of seeing a play on the night of a Rugby international. The city was full of intoxicated Scotsmen, some of whom took a box at the theatre and, fortified with quantities of whisky, completely disrupted the performance.

Sometimes we just wandered about, enjoying the fresh air and the charms of this attractive city, such as the beautiful municipal buildings, the castle grounds and, across the bridge, Sofia Gardens. The old covered market was interesting and photogenic too.

Cardiff was also the regular destination for a young man from one of the other barrack blocks. Most Friday evenings we would watch from our window as he waited outside the WRAF quarters, small suitcase in hand, to greet his girlfriend. They were off to book into a hotel for the weekend as husband and wife. He was a lucky chap; she really was a very pretty girl.

Some evenings we would go to the NAAFI for a drink or perhaps a hot meal, or to the Astra to see a film, but often we would just lounge about in our room. My fellow inhabitants were the usual mixed bunch. Williamson was a chap who managed to stay in bed regularly while the rest of us worked. Our morning parade and march to the workshops was a casual procedure. I once got half-way through the morning before I realised that I was not wearing a collar and tie, and nobody counted the numbers in the electrical shop either. If challenged by the Orderly Officer this layabout would open one eye, mutter "I'm on leave" or something similar and turn over and go to sleep again. Anyone else would have been rumbled but with his sort of bravado he never was. His jacket was notorious too. He had acquired a civilian corduroy blazer in a sickly green colour from someone, already fifth or sixth hand, which had obviously never been dry-cleaned. It smelled and could stand on its own in the corner but he wore it proudly.

'Pedro', whose real name was John, was half Portuguese, a fact that meant that he needn't have been in the services at all, even though he had signed on for fourteen years! He came from a wealthy family in Lisbon. Apparently his English father had taunted him continually about the lack of manliness supposedly arising from not having served in the British armed forces as he himself had done, so 'Pedro' had taken himself off in protest and joined the Royal Air Force.

"Fourteen years! Bit drastic, wasn't it?"

"Well yes, on reflection."

"What do you miss most, being away from home so long?"

"Shafting the maid-servants, mostly. It's a customary privilege of being the son of the house."

'Hank', so nicknamed after a popular writer of semi-pornographic novels, decorated the entire full-length inside of his locker door with photographs of naked females in various artistic poses. I'm not quite sure how, but they survived all inspections, usually with appreciative comments. Another lad had recently returned from a posting to Southern Rhodesia (now Zimbabwe).

"I'm going back there to live when I get demobbed," he informed us. "It's an absolute life of luxury. The climate is wonderful and the natives have to do everything for you for hardly any money."

One chap with artistic qualifications was prevailed upon by the manager of the Astra Cinema to produce regular large-scale display posters illustrating the next week's attraction with an appropriate descriptive comment. 'Hans Christian Anderson', for example, would be subtitled 'The classic fairy stories brought to life'. Unfortunately he never got to see any advance publicity or précis, merely a title, but all went well until he described one film as a 'Stirring Sea Epic', illustrated accordingly, which turned out to be a domestic comedy.

Then there was the man who shot the loud-speaker. Each barrack room was provided with a speaker over the door with the fret-saw logo 'Tannoy', relaying music from the camp radio station. During the evenings you could pop over to this building, slip a request through the letter box and go back and listen to it being played (in fact, it was usually something else, as the record collection was modest). The announcer on duty was supposed to exercise some discretion, although he did once play 'Love for Sale' "in gratitude for the occupants of the WRAF block." One record was aired ad nauseam until someone finally exploded, took up an air pistol and 'killed' the speaker. After a discreet interval we reported it as not working properly, denying any knowledge of the odd holes in it.

Trips home were infrequent. On the way back they in-volved getting up to London, across to Paddington and by late train to Cardiff, arriving there at about three in the morning. On the English side of the Severn rail tunnel it was usually fine weather and on the Welsh pouring with rain. The 'Llantwit Flyer', a long-funnelled museum piece, stood at the 'local' platform, but did not get up steam and depart until six-thirty. Throughout the winter we huddled in a compart-ment, frozen to the core.

One disadvantage of being at St Athan was a reduction to the effective amount of leave that could be taken. All regular serving men were granted 30 days leave a year plus a number of 48-hour passes. It was always emphasised that leave of any kind was a privilege, not a right, and that you were on duty at all times, including weekends, unless otherwise authorised. The interpretation of the regulations was entirely at the discretion of the Commanding Officer. At Harpur Hill the custom had been to apply for five days leave and tack a '48-hours' on both ends of it. Thus you could have a nine-day break six times a year. However, the St Athan CO decreed that leave could only be taken in minimum periods of ten days, including the weekend that these embraced; even starting with a '48' this gave only about a week and a half on only three occasions annually.

Seeking further pleasant distraction for my spare time I joined the church choir, as I had sung in my local place of worship since boyhood. The station church was a brick edifice designed for the purpose, attached to which was a meeting room for the Church Fellowship and I soon found myself involved with that. It was as much a social club as a religious one, where men and women of all ranks, together with civilians on camp, got together for a laugh and a bit of a sing-song, performed a few sketches and generally let their hair down. This opportunity of friendly association with higher ranks was otherwise almost unheard of. Normally no officer or non-commissioned officer would unbend as far as to engage in a normal exchange of small talk with inferiors. Everyone had to remember his status in the chain of command, on or off duty. If a mate was promoted, even to the lowest NCO rank of corporal, he took his meals and leisure with his equals and dropped former friendships.

The leading light in the Fellowship was the padre. Padre Bennett was not everyone's idea of a clergyman, or indeed of a commissioned officer. He was, by any standards, a bit of a lad, and led us in all our less-than-serious activities. He had a fund of hilarious anecdotes and slightly improper songs and could always be prevailed upon to give us a few verses of his latest ditty about events and personalities on camp, accompanying himself on a banjo. This 'character' owned a character's car, an ancient open-topped vehicle that may once have been a convertible. The upholstery was mouldy and the bodywork pitted all over. According to him it had accidentally been dropped in the Red Sea while being loaded onto a ship on the way back from Aden.

One day a bunch of us saw him negotiating the camp entrance and stalling it. We jeered and cat-called to him as he good-naturedly got us to push it. A passing Warrant Officer stared in disbelief at a group of airmen addressing a Squadron Leader in such a manner. Of course he was an officer by virtue of his calling and not through any wish to emulate his equals, as could be seen by his bearing when on parade. He couldn't march at all. Called upon to ascend a rostrum and conduct a prayer, he loped across in a rather affected and uncoordinated manner, arms all over the place. Most people therefore considered him a bit of a joke; he was, in fact, a smashing bloke. At one stage he decided that the Fellowship should engage in a bit of evangelism. I was a bit uncomfortable about this for although I had always been a church attender I didn't claim much in the way of religious fervour, being more interested in the singing. Nevertheless, in pairs we were sent off round the houses of the married quarters to attempt a bit of converting. Fortunately, my companion, a WRAF sergeant called Mary, was very devout, bordering on religious mania, so she did all the talking while I drank all the tea. A story circulated that she made herself so objectionable with her constant preaching in the Sergeants' Mess that the male NCOs finally hung her up on coat hooks in the entrance hall by the shoulder loops on her battledress and left her there a long time for passers-by to prod.

There were several nice girls in the Fellowship and I became friendly with one called Pat, who took me home to meet her parents in married quarters, a somewhat uneasy experience as I attempted conversation with her father aimed to be somewhere between friendly discussion and the deference due to a Warrant Officer. Pat and I went on walks together, mostly accompanied by her sister and others of the Fellowship, perhaps strolling down to Llantwit Major beach. We would sometimes catch the train to Barry, where she once embarrassed me by knocking on doors in the main street and running away. She was only about seventeen. Frequently we changed trains there onto the short branch line to Barry Island, which was lively in the summer, with its seaside amusements and fairground but which, like most resorts, looked sad and abandoned in winter with the fair closed and all stalls and side-shows boarded up. The one place that stayed open throughout was the roller-skating rink, where I learned numerous ways of falling over.

Sometimes a group of us went to the regular dance which took place in the East Camp in a large hangar. This was a big affair with a good band, subdued lighting and plenty of drink. A member of our camera club used to circulate among the dancers and those sitting out, taking photographs of the various couples and groups, for subsequent purchase, and very good they were. We were very intrigued with his equipment. He was shooting off shot after shot, all with the aid of flashlight, without constantly discarding and replacing bulbs, which is what was normally expected. What he was using, he explained, was one of the new electronic flash guns. It required a wire from the lamp unit on the camera to run down to a heavy power pack the size of a small suitcase suspended at his side on a shoulder strap.

An official duty, which came round regularly, for those following my trade, was Duty Electrician. This involved being on call throughout twenty-four hours, armed with a small toolkit, ready to solve any electrical problem, large or small, that might crop up anywhere on the premises, and praying that it would not be a major fault in important equipment such as that in use in the mess halls, which would have been beyond our basic abilities. In fact, I was called out on two occasions. Firstly, I was summoned to the home of a Flying Officer in married quarters, where the lights had all gone off. To begin with, he sternly refused permission for me to inspect the fuses, which he assured me were satisfactory, and only with some difficulty, under the authority he had over my humble rank, was I able to prove him wrong and restore the power. Another time I was requested to report to the 'waffery', to the amusement of my colleagues. At the door I was met by the WRAF sergeant and told to wait until she had got her charges safely into their dormitories and all decently attired. She preceded me up to the top floor, calling out on each landing "Warning! Man in the block!" to a response of much girlish giggling. My attention was directed to a small incinerator on the wall by the toilets which had ceased to operate. I soon traced the fault to loose wiring and corrected it before being led down again under the same tight restrictions.

"What do you actually incinerate in it?" I asked the sergeant. All I got was a suppressed smile and an order to be dismissed.

When I had been at St Athan for about three months, I started to think about promotion. I still had about two-and-a-half years' service before me and didn't want to spend them all as an AC1. Also, I reasoned, the higher the rank the better it would be later on in seeking a job. The next step up would be LAC (Leading Aircraftman) and then SAC (Senior Aircraftman). After that on the technical ladder came Junior Technician and Senior Technician, sporting single or double stripes similar to corporals, but upside-down to indicate technical ranks. Having swotted up a bit, I put my name down for and sat the examination at LAC level. The names of those who had passed were posted on a noticeboard. Mine was not among them. After another three months I applied again and was informed that I had, in fact, been successful the first time but needed the appropriate education qualification. Apparently my School Certificate had somehow not been recorded on my records, so again I sent home for it. My promotion was then granted with an increase in income and a nice lump sum in several months of back-dated pay.

Rank badges with the two-bladed propellers on them were drawn from stores and sewn on all sleeves. Most of us soon became proficient with our needles and could sew back a button in no time. Socks were in constant need of darning and some of us acquired a little gadget that the NAAFI sold that resembled a tiny loom, which overfilled the hole with a woven square patch. This resulted in a thickish area which was not very comfortable. Before long I did some more reading and sat and passed the examination for SAC, replacing the badges with the three-bladed propeller version.

There were, of course, medical facilities available and we endured the usual occasional humiliation of the FFI inspection. Fortunately I never had to consult the Medical Officer, a complicated and deliberately off-putting procedure, but I did go to the dentist. He was a very young Pilot Officer, no doubt fresh out of training, who did not inspire much confidence. Digging a hole in my aching tooth, he put in a temporary filling, indicating that it would be replaced permanently when he was certain that no further decay had occurred. Twice more I went back to have it dug out and replaced with the same story. I never did get rid of that temporary filling while at St Athan. At intervals the Blood Donor people paid a visit and we were bribed to volunteer in return for an extra forty-eight hour pass. There were lots of donors.

Service life continued its largely monotonous course, broken occasionally with such necessary interruptions as parades or kit inspections, so once again I flouted the airmen's unofficial law and volunteered for a few opportunities to do something a bit different. The east coast of England was suffering from disastrous floods and volunteers were called upon to go there to fill sandbags and help in all manner of ways with repairing sea defences and other results of the disaster. Members of the forces were released for this duty, starting with those closest to the smitten area and working west. The need for assistance never reached Wales so I didn't have to go.

On 24th March 1953 'old' Queen Mary, the widow of King George the Fifth, died and many shop windows in Cardiff were decked out with black drapes and photographs of the lady. This occurred less than three months before the coronation of the new queen was to take place and in connection with that once more volunteers were sought, to participate in the events of this momentous occasion. This would involve secondment for three weeks to a camp for special preparation, culminating in forming part of the continuous line of military personnel bordering every part of the route that the

Royal procession would take through London on June the second, Coronation Day. This time I was selected for duty, along with many others, and set off for training at RAF Aston Down in Gloucestershire in preparation for the Coronation.

6. Aston Down and The Coronation

We were met at Stroud railway station and conveyed in lorries to the Royal Air Force base at Aston Down. This was, or had been, a flying unit with a runway, acres of concrete and a hard perimeter road circling the camp. There were large numbers of us preparing for the Coronation duties, housed in huts and sleeping in two-tier bunks to maximise space.

Rifles were issued for the duration of training and the actual day. These were suspended under the top bunk on webbing straps when not in use and were hard on the skull when the lower occupant sat up in bed. Our normal skewer-like bayonets were replaced with an impressive long, wide-bladed version. The atmosphere was pleasant and we were well looked after, the food being the best I had sampled at any location so far. An early requirement was for us to be measured for special uniforms that would be tailor-made to fit properly, a novel experience.

The three-weeks training started fairly gently and gradually intensified. My group's Route Lining 'station' on the day was going to be in Piccadilly Circus. On a large area of tarmac a representation of this area was marked out accurately, full size, in white paint, showing the pavement edges and the location of such landmarks as Eros, Swan and Edgar's emporium, the London Pavilion, the top corner of The Haymarket and the curved approach from Regent Street. Repeatedly we practised arriving at precisely the right spot and dressing an arm's length from the next man. We brushed up familiar drill movements until we moved as one body in mechanical precision and added a few new variations, including lunch arrangements. There was going to be a considerable wait before the procession passed us and lunch boxes would be placed by our feet, so we learned how, on command, to 'take up lunch boxes'.

Our temporary home in the capital was going to be a tented area in Kensington Gardens, some two and a half miles from our place on the processional route, so we had to prepare for this by marching for increasing distances until we could get right round the airfield perimeter, an equivalent mileage, and take up position near 'Eros' without discomfort. This march would have to be undertaken with the rifles in the slope-arms position, an impossible strain on the left arms, so we learned a procedure for 'changing arms on the march' to the other shoulder and back again at intervals. Removing an unfamiliar bayonet from behind, fixing it to the rifle, unfixing it and returning it to its frog, frequently led to embarrassment at first, but we practised until it was executed perfectly.

"It's going to be a bright sunny day on June the second," we were assured. But, just in case, we had to learn a rain drill. Part of our standard kit was a groundsheet which doubled as a cape and which we folded into a neat roll fixed behind us to our webbing belt with straps. Some time was spent on a drill to remove this garment and fix it round the neck. As we might be required to do this while on the march, with rifle in the left hand, we attempted this with one hand only. On the command 'trail arms' we lowered the rifle to arm's length. On other commands we found the neck of the cape, pulled it sharply from its fixings, held it aloft to open it and with the right hand only flung it round the neck and fastened the button. That was the theory. Needless to say this difficult task mostly defeated us but, as the sergeant said, we were promised fine weather.

Some evenings were spent in nearby Stroud, where there were plenty of young ladies; very young, most of them.

"Why are there so many sixteen-year-old girls here?" someone asked.

"Perhaps the randy troops preparing for the last Coronation were stationed here; that was seventeen years ago!"

Time passed and we received our uniforms, fitting perfectly and made from a fine material like the officers', together with smart peaked caps. Obviously we couldn't appear on such an important occasion in our normal coarse serge and beret like a potato sack.

"You'll be the envy of your mates when you get back to your camps," we were told, "and there's going to be a special Coronation medal struck."

On Coronation eve we were trucked down to Stroud station to be 'entrained', after which an officer came along the platform and carefully locked every compartment door from the outside, to our alarm.

"I've had to sign for this bloody train," he said. "You will be let out at the other end when I'm quite sure it's in the condition it was when I assumed responsibility for it."

That train was specially routed and on approaching London wandered off onto various little-used tracks covered in nettles and into several tunnels before finally pulling up at the platform of Lancaster Gate Underground station!

Across the road in Kensington Gardens were more ridge tents than could ever have been assembled in one place before. There seemed to be thousands of them, extending as far as the eye could see. We had to find a vacant one and memorise its position, there being no row numbers to help us. As long as you remembered that you were in, say, the twenty-ninth tent down the thirty-sixth row, you could find your way back; otherwise you were lost! The tent contained nothing but a floor of slatted duckboards and we were directed to obtain and stuff a palliasse. A large marquee was filled with loose straw and human bodies. We had to pick up a sack, enter the marquee and fill this. What with the condition of the straw and the effect of many feet trampling through it, you could hardly see for dust. So we emerged with red noses and running eyes and blew black particles into our handkerchiefs for several days. I hoped that nobody suffered from hay fever.

There were also a number of other large canvas structures serving as dining area, toilets and washing facilities and even a lounge with a large-screen projector television in it. The logistics of organising all this for thousands of us must have been horrific, and it was just our RAF lot; further away were camped vast numbers of military personnel of all service branches and nationalities. And all over London, in The Mall and open spaces, hundreds and thousands of civilian visitors were camped out in the open air all night to claim a view-point for the big event.

It was a belief generally circulating that anyone in uniform in London at that time would be treated to free drinks in pubs in the evening through the generosity of the millions of tourists and foreign visitors and some of us decided to get into the West End and test out this theory. Fighting our way onto the Underground we set out for Oxford Circus and made our way down Regent Street, ultimately to Trafalgar Square. Some of my companions were seeing the actual statue of Eros and the venue for the next day's duties for the first time. The crowds were already filling the pavements with some preparing to stay where they were all night. It was all very genial and good-natured but we pushed into several licensed establishments and no-one bought us anything.

On our return to Kensington Gardens we stripped and attempted to get comfortable on our palliasses, which proved impossible. Perhaps we hadn't stuffed them properly but nothing seemed to stop the duck-boards digging into our hips. Sleep came slowly and fitfully, interrupted for most of the night by revellers returning. Several times, befuddled lost souls would undo the bottom few loops of the tent flap, poke a head through and enquire "Nobby (or Fred or George, etc) are you in there?"

"No he isn't. Piss off!"

Ah well, it was only for two nights!

Up on the big day bright and early, we washed and shaved, breakfasted, put the final touches to our nice new uniforms, boots and webbing, and set off on our route march. Passing along the north side of Kensington Gardens and Hyde Park, alive with multi-coloured uniforms from all parts of the globe, we marched through the gates of Marble Arch, in itself a rare privilege. Along Oxford Street and down Regent Street the crowds packed every inch of pavement and up-stairs windows, cheering each Flight or Squad of military personnel as it passed on the way to take up its route-lining position. Flags and bunting abounded and pictures of Her Majesty were displayed in most shops. Above the main entrance to Selfridge's store stood a magnificent full size effigy of the queen in her full dress uniform on horseback.

At intervals the officer in charge of our Flight gave us the instruction to change arms on the march, which we could now perform in perfect timing upon the sole initial order. Ahead of us, apparently, other squads made up of all kinds of men from all branches of the services, had been still shout-ing out the steps used in training; "Change arms on the march, (pause) One, (pause) Two, (pause) Three, (pause) Four!" which amused the crowds who cheerfully shouted it at us every time we carried it out. It had been drizzling and started to rain more heavily. Our officer came out of for-mation and walked back beside us.

"I'm going to have to give you the order to put on ground-sheets on the march," he warned us, and returned to the front of the column.

"Flight... trail arms!"

We removed the rifles from our shoulders and lowered them.

"Flight... hands on groundsheets!"

"Flight... remove groundsheets!"

We pulled them, still rolled up, out of their straps, with a sharp tug. They were wet, as were our hands, and almost without exception they shot off into the crowd, some of whom donned them gratefully. After that, we just put up with being wet, a nuisance for us but worse for the Marines, who soon had streaks of white blanco running off their helmets and down their faces. In due course the weather improved somewhat.

With precision we arrived at our section of the route in Piccadilly Circus and shuffled into position, rifles at the stand-at-ease position. A good view of the procession was expected as we were all facing the road, not the crowds, as is the security requirement for the police nowadays. However, this would mean a long wait as it was only on the return journey to Buckingham Palace after the ceremony in West-minster Abbey that the procession would take the long way back through the West End during the afternoon. It was not possible to turn round and chat to the cheerful crowds which did not stop them passing remarks to and about us. A few people did not seem to understand quite what was happen-ing. I heard an American lady ask, "This is where we see the Coronation take place, isn't it?" to be told "No, that's in the Abbey."

"Well, what will I see here?"

"The procession."

"Oh!" she said doubtfully.

It is surprisingly easy to faint if you stand locked motionless in one position, as had been demonstrated before sometimes on parade, so occasionally we were brought to attention, sloped arms and marked time on the spot. We were allowed two toilet breaks, one in the morning and one in the afternoon. Alternate men were marched off accordingly, leaving the others to maintain the line and take their turn afterwards. Piccadilly Circus Underground station, which was closed to the public throughout the day, was unlocked for us so we could use the facilities. When we were all done and back in position after the morning break there was a conspicuous gap in the ranks. One chap, presumably closeted on longer business than the rest of us, had got himself locked in the Underground and wasn't rescued until the afternoon shift went in. As lunchtime approached, members of an army corps appeared, pulling hand carts and receiving a great cheer from the multitude. They placed a square cardboard box by the feet of every man on parade.

"Attention!" We obeyed.

"Ground Arms!" We lowered our rifles to the road and stood to attention again.

"Take up lunch boxes!" We bent down, picked them up and held them neatly in both hands.

"Open lunch-boxes!" With one hand we folded back the lid.

"Commence lunch!" We started eating.

All of this was met with howls of delight by the public as we consumed our snacks and drinks and went into reverse procedures to return the empty boxes to the ground for re-collection.

Eventually the noise of the crowds back in Regent Street warned us that the great procession was approaching and we were brought to attention again. There were, we were told later, twelve thousand persons in the parade which stretched for two miles from front to rear and took some time to pass. As it prepared to veer to the right past Eros for the turn into The Haymarket we had the most wonderful view of the whole thing passing no more than ten feet in front of us. Troop after troop of soldiers, sailors and airpeople of both sexes and many nationalities marched through, accompanied by bands and pipers. The Commonwealth was fully represented in varied and colourful uniforms, including the magnificent Canadian 'Mounties'. Leaders of the armed forces, past and present, including General Montgomery, came by in horse-drawn coaches and Heads of State, including the wonderful Queen Salote of Tonga, who endeared herself to everybody by her obvious enjoyment in an open carriage in the rain. She was accompanied by a small man, presumably an aide. Reputedly a friend said to Noel Coward, "What is that small man beside her?" The appearance of this diminutive figure accompanying the very large lady from the South Pacific islands is supposed to have prompted The Master to reply "Her lunch!"

More open coaches brought us the newly-styled Queen Mother, Princess Margaret, Winston Churchill and other familiar figures. The men in particular looked remarkably healthy in the overcast light and I am quite sure that they were using cosmetics, perhaps for the benefit of all the colour film cameras. The golden State Coach was a wonderful sight behind its team of immaculate horses and footmen, and the young Queen Elizabeth II was radiant and beautiful.

Eventually the exuberance of the crowds subsided and they could rest their throats while we, in reverse order, waited our turn to form up and march back to our temporary accommodation.

After a meal, many of us crowded into the lounge tent to see some of the day's events repeated, in black and white of course, on the large-screen television. Memorable were the shots taken from the top of Marble Arch, looking down Park Lane. The camera showed a wide view of the procession, then appeared to move in closer and closer for a look at individual personalities. The only way we knew for a camera to bring you apparently nearer from a static location was for a different lens to be selected and television cameras usually had a turret with several lenses of differing focal length on them. Obviously a way had been found of varying focal length on one lens; I was seeing, for the first time, the effect of a zoom lens, and quite spectacular it seemed.

The next day we entrained again and detrained in Gloucestershire. To our great disappointment we had to give back our nice new uniforms and caps. Goodness knows where they all went. Some discussion took place about our missing ground-sheets and it was decided that it would not be practicable to put us all on a charge or, in all fairness, to make us pay for lost kit.

And so, after a really wonderful experience, we all returned to mundane life at our various 'home' stations.

Soon after our return to St Athan we asked about the distribution of the Coronation Medal. We learned that a number had been sent to each RAF station to be allotted at the Commanding Officer's discretion. Ours had given them to himself and other 'deserving' high-ranking officers, none of whom had had anything to do with the celebrations. We felt, with some justification, that at least *some* of those who had contributed to the magnificence of the Coronation should have been considered.

Not long afterwards the Queen paid an official visit to the town of Newport, some 25 miles down the road and a Guard of Honour was required, which provided another opportunity for some of us to brush up our drill and turn out on parade. As we presented arms, Her Majesty gave a gracious wave in our direction.

"Oh, look at that," someone whispered, "she remembers us from the second of June!" The event was on a small scale but offered another break in our routine existence.

Having been at St Athan for almost exactly a year, I was unexpectedly given an overseas posting. I was advised to use up some of my outstanding leave allocation, so spent ten days at home, saying goodbye to friends and family. Overseas terms of service were usually for two years, about the time I had left to complete, so it would almost certainly be the summer of 1955 before I could see them again. The only overseas place we knew of from where you could make home visits was Gibraltar, but this was classed as a 'home' posting. An overseas destination really meant somewhere further afield, although the location was not imparted to me. Very soon after that, I was awarded a week's 'embarkation leave', extra to standard annual privilege, so surprised everybody at home by saying goodbye to them all over again! I also took my leave of all my friends on camp, performed the ritual of signing out and departed for Lytham St Anne's in Lancashire, where preparations for foreign duty took place.

Over the next few days, along with several hundred other men on their way to exotic locations, I was kitted out and inoculated. The kit, to be carried in an extra small kitbag, included light brown tropical bush-jackets, shorts, long trousers, khaki socks and peaked caps. To add to our collection of items never to be used was an enamel mess plate, a water bottle and a pair of sunglasses in a case. The 'jabs', spread over several days, were to protect us from any dirty foreign bugs, including some that we had never heard of.

During the evenings some of us investigated the delights of Blackpool, a short bus ride away. In the Tower building we rode to the top to see the famous second sunset, which takes place after the one at ground level, sampled the drinks at the 'longest bar in the country' and wandered into the ballroom to watch the dancers. Reginald Dixon, the distinguished resident organist, was seated at his white Mighty Wurlitzer, bathed in brilliant spotlight. At the other side of the stage a pure white grand piano, coupled to the organ console, appeared to be playing itself. Outside, we explored the fairground and wandered along the Golden Mile, with its various stalls and side-shows. A rather flashy blonde in charge of a rifle range engaged us in conversation. All of us were in uniform as we had been obliged to jettison our 'civvies' before leaving the country.

"Where are you posted to, lads?" she asked.

"Posted to?" we countered cautiously, as we had been told that troop movements were a classified matter. The most that we had discovered was that we would be attached to MEAF (Middle East Air Force) which embraced a large area of the globe from the central Mediterranean through to India. Quite possibly some of us would end up in the place reputed to be the largest RAF station in the world, RAF Habbaniyah in Iraq, or at the hottest, RAF Khormaksar in Aden.

"Come off it!" she said. "You are up at Lytham, aren't you?"

"Well, yes..."

"What hut are you in?"

"Um, 6D actually."

"Then you're off to RAF Fayid."

"Where's that?"

"In the Suez Canal Zone."

"Silly cow!" we muttered as we wandered off. "How could she possibly know?"

There followed a couple of days on 'Pool Flight', doing the rounds of the dustbins, then we were off to spend one night at RAF Hendon in North London. This was close enough for yet another quick home visit so, with a new pal, I caught a Green Line bus and turned up again on the doorstep.

"Just when we keep thinking that we've seen the back of you!" my father said, with a twinkle. My mother was a bit subdued.

In the morning we were roused early, loaded into coaches with our two kitbags each and conveyed out to Stansted, which was a very modest airfield in those days. On the tarmac stood our transport, an old Dakota with the logo of Scottish Airways on its fuselage. This was, in fact, on loan to Transport Command and the 'air steward' was a young airman. His pre-flight talk was somewhat unnerving, since hardly any of us had ever flown before. It went something like this:

> "Now this is a Dakota. Most of them reach their destination OK. The pilot's got a parachute but you haven't, so I hope if we come down on water you can swim. Mind you, the engines don't usually pack up together; well, they haven't for the last week or so. Under your seat is a lifejacket. It takes five minutes to put it on. We've usually hit the water in three. To evacuate the plane of all passengers takes about fifteen minutes but unfortunately it sinks in ten! In front of you will be found a sick-bag. I can't remember whether they have been emptied since yesterday."

He retired to his cubicle, chuckling at his own wit, while the more susceptible among us looked very thoughtful.

It took two full days in four legs to get to our destination, which was good compared to some troop movements which were still being undertaken by sea. Once we were airborne the steward handed round cans of beer, with no means of opening them. Penknives were produced and the tops pierced. Owing, I suppose, to the cabin conditions the liquid, mostly as foam, shot up and festooned itself along the ceiling. After about four hours we landed at Nice for refuelling and something to eat, which we took without leaving the terminal. "Yes, I've been to France", I used to say.

By the way, for all this foreign travel and more to come, none of the service personnel ever needed a passport.

In the afternoon another four hours or so brought us to RAF Luqa in Malta, where we drew from a store a supply of bedding for one night in the extravagantly styled 'Airmen's Transit Hotel'. After a meal several adventurous spirits suggested taking a taxi into the capital Valletta to sample the attractions of The Gut, which apparently included intoxicating beverages and ladies of a certain type. The proper name of this notorious location is Strait Street and it has now lost much of its former reputation. This wasn't my scene and anyway we had to be up fairly early in the morning, so I declined. This didn't prevent a disturbed night as the revellers returned, somewhat the worse for wear, in the small hours.

In the morning we donned, as instructed, our new bush-jackets and the long trousers. The best thing about this uniform was the fact that it did not require an undershirt, collar and tie. Once again we took to the air and I could claim having visited another foreign country, or at least its airport.

By lunchtime I could add another, Libya, as we landed for yet more refuelling at a place that seemed to be a collection of buildings completely surrounded by sand, called El Adem. The final leg, mostly over desert, brought us to a sandy runway that was obviously part of a large Royal Air Force establishment.

Where were we?

RAF Fayid, in the Canal Zone, in Egypt, of course.

7. Suez Canal Zone, Egypt

We didn't stay at RAF Fayid but were moved off some miles south, in lorries, to a camp with transit facilities. These must have been fully occupied for we were put in a gymnasium to spend the night on mattresses on the floor. After inspecting the NAAFI we settled down but the heat made sleep difficult and we hoped for the temperature to fall; it didn't much. Someone gasped and drew our attention to a couple of beetles crawling round between the mattresses. They were about ten times the size of the good old UK models and, for all we knew, injurious to health. That kept us awake for a bit, too.

Next day we were appointed to our various establishments. With a small group of others I was transported back by the previous evening's route through the narrow tract of cultivated land alongside the Suez Canal to within a short distance of the airfield; in fact, to the camp next door, 109 MU RAF Abyad, MEAF 25, which served as a Maintenance Unit and was to be the final posting of my service career.

It was possible to familiarise ourselves with the surroundings in our bit of Egypt only slowly over the next few months as we gradually explored places that were 'in bounds'. The Suez Canal Zone, some one hundred miles in length, was teeming with British personnel of the various services, in dozens of individual camps. Some of these establishments were clustered in garrison areas such as Moascar near Ismailia and Fayid, not far from the Great Bitter Lake, which lies about two thirds of the distance south from Port Said. Nobody ever briefed us on the reasons for this massive presence and we knew nothing of the political background and animosity to the foreign occupation. We assumed that we were there to safeguard the international status of the waterway and to protect our own units, probably not from military action but from the activities of some of the natives who frequently broke into camps to steal such things as cigarettes and spirits from the canteens and had been known to attack, and even on one occasion kill, officials for the contents of their wallets.

Abyad, with its familiar collection of buildings such as barracks, stores, NAAFI, cinema, YMCA, cookhouse, workshops and so on, was spread over a considerable area. New arrivals, identified by the pale appearance of their legs, were accommodated in a permanent tented area, from which it took a year or so to graduate to a brick hut. At a glance there were rows of identical ridge tents, each housing three men. On closer inspection it was evident that efforts had been made by the occupants to give them some individuality. Most had been floored over with discarded boarding from packing cases and some sported signs outside with 'Mon Repos', 'Dunroamin' or the like on them. Others, including B4, the one to which I was directed, had been taken to great lengths to make them a 'home-from-home'.

The sand beneath them, which under the surface was quite firm, had been dug down to form a square hole the area of the tent and about two foot six in depth and this had been lined around the walls as well as on the bottom with the wooden panelling. On this floor, in our case, was laid a carpet fashioned from the thick felt that had once lined crates of aircraft parts. Three specially-made slim cupboards supported the tent poles, so that the tent was at normal height above ground. This increased standing room from just the centre to the whole interior. Steps up to the surface were cut out and lined and the lockers and beds, with their mosquito nets, arranged in a more satisfactory layout. All this was tolerated by the authorities as long as proper attention to neatness and cleanliness was observed. Cables ran round the site under the sand providing electricity to each tent for the sole purpose of powering a light bulb.

As soon as I had drawn the usual items of bedding from Stores and settled in, I was invited by my two new companions to contribute my one-third share towards the radio. A long time earlier one of the residents had 'acquired' this set and it had been sold on from one to another ever since.

"Where is it?" I asked.

"It is in here; have a look for it." I couldn't find it. The others rolled back a corner of the carpet and prised up a square of the flooring. Beneath was a further small excavation containing this highly illegal piece of equipment, connected to the power supply via a cable spliced into the mains somewhere under the sand. It had come out of an aircraft and was not designed for high fidelity music reproduction. High across the length of the tent was strung a wire, ostensibly for hanging clothes on but also serving as an aerial. Tuned into the Services Broadcasting Station, only a short distance away, the set's performance was just about acceptable. It was almost as good tuned into London and we used to listen to 'Take it from Here' both direct from the BBC and locally off discs of earlier episodes flown out from London. There were many locally produced broadcasts, including commentary on inter-service sporting events, quizzes recorded at various service canteens and family and children's programmes for the married quarters people. Very popular were the record sessions, airing requests received from contacts at home or the forces themselves. Greatly in demand was the Harry Roy Orchestra's 'She Had to go and Lose it at The Astor' which we all thought was rude. It couldn't have been, though, because as the last line explains, "All they did was stand and gape;

there was Minnie's sable cape, and she thought that she had lost it at The Astor."

As well as unauthorised radios, in some tents there were also various home-made contrivances such as heaters for water or toast. Some time after my arrival our superiors noticed that the power, as metered into the tented area, showed an alarming usage in excess of that expected from a few light bulbs and ordered an investigation. Who carried it out? Why, electricians of course, i.e. some of *us*. We knew where it was going but we poked about all over the place with our little meters and reported that as far as we could tell the modestly insulated cables must be leaking power under the sand!

I committed two sins on my first evening in my new surroundings. With another newcomer I wandered down to sample the delights of the airmen's bar in the NAAFI. This single-storey complex had a small garden full of exotic foliage that trailed over trellis arches on an approach path. Plants could only be made to flourish in that desert terrain with constantly running water and plenty of attention but when they did they usually made a spectacular show. There were no signs by the door so we marched in, only to be caught under the armpits by a corporal who marched us out again.

"Where do you think you are going?"

"The NAAFI, aren't we?"

"This is the Junior NCO's bar. Yours is round the corner. And furthermore I could put you on a charge for being improperly dressed."

We stared at him. What we had done, apparently, contrary to Standing Orders, was to remain in our day-time shorts when we ought to have changed into long trousers at dusk, presumably on account of the mosquitoes. Our bar was a dingy and completely functional place. The ceiling was completely covered in silvery pellets of some sort. It seemed that it was customary on removing the foil from the inside of a cigarette packet to screw it into a ball, chew it until it was heavy and adhesive, and heave it up aloft.

If we had waited another half hour or so we should have had no difficulty in identifying the airmen's bar by the noise emanating from it. There being very little else to do, many men spent their entire evenings in there, getting increasingly incapable and rowdy. Nowhere could there have been consumed greater quantities of the local 'Stella' brand of beer, which was reputed to be brewed from onions. I can't vouch for it myself but it was said that the taste of them began to emerge after about eight pints. So very soon each night the raucous bellowing of vulgar songs would start up:

We were leaving Khartoum by the light of the moon.
We travelled by night and by day.
We passed Kasfareet, we'd had fuck-all to eat;
We'd given our rations away.

Or:

Queen Farida, queen of all the wogs;
Queen Farida, shagged by all the dogs.
Queen Farida's gone away
'cause she's in the family way!

Two points of etiquette require comment. I'm not going to keep on using the most controversial of the four-letter words, but the fact is that it was employed all the time in that boring virtually men-only environment. Everybody, even the good little boys, gradually absorbed this manner of speech until we all used it all the time without even noticing. To have refrained would have been eccentric. It was inserted into almost every sentence without thought and even into the middle of words. Absofuckinglutely. The other point concerns the word 'wog' which causes so much offence. We used the word with as much thought behind it as we gave to our unconventional language. The origins of the term are much debated but we were led to believe that it arose a long time in the past from capital letters stencilled on native employees' overalls to denote that they were 'Working On Government Service'. A less likely suggestion was that they were 'Westernised Oriental Gentlemen'.

There were on camp large numbers of native civilians, serving in bars and shops, labouring in workshops and acting as 'bearers' in the billets by polishing shoes and other menial tasks. They were, in all honesty, mostly from the very bottom of the social ladder, living in the village across the road from the main gate, in mud huts with no doors or windows and not by any means typifying the lifestyle in other parts of the land. This village, like a number in the Zone, was not a traditional historic settlement but had sprung up for the convenience of those hoping for employment.

Past this village ran a waterway called The Sweet Water Canal, part of Egypt's ancient transport network, and so inappropriately named to distinguish it from the salty Suez Canal nearby. It wasn't very sweet, being used for all domestic purposes, including waste, and in fact if any of us should be unlucky enough to fall in it, we were told, it would mean hospitalisation and a cocktail of strong counter-measures. However, it was common to see a villager up to his armpits in the water, fully dressed, in an attempt at bathing, while another man on the bank crouched with his rear end over the edge, defecating. Further downstream someone might be dipping a kettle into the same water for making tea.

Many of these locals were paid a wage by the British but had no concept of its use. During the winter it could be surprisingly chilly, especially at night, and our blood had been thinned throughout the hot summer. We changed into 'blues' during the colder months but you might find that Mohammed or Ahmed was missing in the morning, having died of cold. They were never greatly perturbed by these tragedies, everything occurring through divine will.

Some of the village boys had one disfigured eyeball, allegedly poked deliberately to render them unsuitable for military service, which would have taken them away from their role in helping and supporting their parents. In what little areas of cultivation that existed adjacent to the waterways we could see that agricultural methods had not moved since biblical times. It was made clear to us that most of the places where these poor people lived were strictly 'out of bounds'.

The villagers made full use of the clapped-out local taxis. Frequently one would arrive in the rough space in front of the village. The passengers clinging on the running boards would get off and anything up to six more would emerge from the inside so that several others could alight. All the rest would get back on somehow, together with any newcomers, and the vehicle would grind off in a cloud of dust with much waving and voluble Arabic. Down the road, at a level (!) crossing, it was possible to see that there was no limit on the capacity of railway carriages either, as the trains went through loaded to the windows, with more bodies clinging onto the roof.

Yet again I found myself languishing in an under-utilised workshop during working hours, although to my surprise someone at last noticed that my civilian occupation had related to refrigeration systems. One job that did occur occasionally was the installation and maintenance of portable air-conditioning units. Important buildings were equipped with cooling ducting. The refrigerated air for this was provided by units on two-wheeled trailers that stood outside on the verandas. These sometimes needed an overhaul or repair, a task that I was able to do. Several times they had to be collected from and returned to various RAF sites, either towed behind a lorry or, in the case of several at a time, by means of a Queen Mary, an extra-long articulated low-loader designed for aircraft wings and fuselages. This gave me an occasional opportunity to see a little of the country-side in the narrow, somewhat fertile strip alongside the Suez and Sweet Water canals, and compare my camp with others.

There was a small contingent of WRAFs living well apart from rough men in their own heavily guarded quarters. One day one of these turned up to augment the technicians in the workshop. It was half-way through the morning before we realised that our language might perhaps be modified, by which time we noticed that this hard-bitten young lady could out-swear us all.

Work was carried out, or not, in long morning sessions, the afternoons being considered too hot. Our inclination was to lounge about on our beds during the heat of the afternoon but before long a couple of us decided that we ought to explore further afield. This always took some determination.

"Fancy going out?" A long pause.

"Fancy going out?" Another.

"It means putting on a few clothes."

"I know."

"It's a long trudge to the main gate."

It was; over of a quarter of a mile I should think.

"I know. It'll rain." This of course was the standard joke.

Having made the effort we presented ourselves for in-spection at the guardroom and left the camp. Among the few options open to us at first was the Fayid Shopping Centre, a mile or two down the Treaty Road. Longer excursions were considered a bit risky, although as the situation eased later on we could venture further away. Transport was available in the form of CABS. These were not taxis but the Canal Army

Bus Service, being army lorries fitted out with steps at the back and painted in a livery of blue and white. A soldier with a rifle rode on the back step and we ourselves always had to be in pairs while out of camp. We climbed aboard at the stop right outside the gate and the lorry shot off down the rutted road, bumped over the level crossing and deposited us in the shopping village. This was a fairly smart complex of shops in several streets, built in the local sandstone by and for the British service personnel and serving the whole Fayid garrison. Some foliage had been persuaded to grow and an ornamental fountain stood at the crossroads, giving the place an attractive appearance. The tenant shopkeepers were natives and the whole area was under the watchful eyes of the Military Police patrolling at all times. There were a number of good shops and cafés with grandiose 'English' names such as The Grand Auberge, The Oxford Tailor, John Bull's and Freddie Mills' Emporium, including an excellent camera shop and a NAAFI with a nursery and a grocery for the ladies of the various married quarters.

On the perimeter of this area the street traders abounded, with whom we soon learned the art of bargaining. Something, a watch perhaps, would be offered, the price lowered repeatedly upon each rejection until it was only a fraction of the original demand. This was not necessarily a bargain though; a wristwatch appearing to be bursting with jewels and giving all manner of information including the phases of the moon could usually be guaranteed to work for about a week. These casual traders addressed us in fractured English and we countered with the few words of Arabic that we soon learned, undoubtedly used and pronounced incorrectly but apparently understood.

"Shufti." (Let's have a look.)

"Kam feloose?" (How much?)

"Le; le; le!" (No; no; no!)

"Mafeesh feloose." (I've got no money.)

"Imshi!" (Go away!)

"Imshi yallah! (Definitely go away!)

Close at hand was a large army cinema and, as we discovered on subsequent trips, a further short walk brought you to the shore of the Great Bitter Lake, where a service canteen served cool drinks and food. Here you could swim in an area cordoned off from the lake by several old barges that had been scuttled to form a rectangular pool hopefully cut off from the occasional shark that found its way there from the Red Sea, the Suez Canal having no locks. Removing shoes, you had to run like hell for the water to avoid burning the soles of your feet on the sand and when in it you might step on something quite revoltingly squishy. As might be expected the water in the lake was extremely salty, leaving a taste in the mouth and a white deposit on the skin. One of the waiters in the canteen, in his long *jellaba* and turban, regularly played a little game. This involved removing your empty Coca-Cola bottle at the precise moment that you had emptied it, no earlier and no later. He did this without hovering and we used to try and catch him out by keeping half an inch back until he was out of sight then draining it quickly. Without fail, as soon as the bottle touched the table it was lifted off with a triumphant gleam.

The road to this pleasant amenity passed through a tiny village, of quite the most disgusting nature, for the locals' own use. Open-fronted mud structures served as shops, including one trading as a butcher's that usually had an unidentifiable carcass with a long hairy tail hanging on a hook, surrounded by a swarm of flies. This seemed to remain there for weeks on end, reducing gradually in size as pieces were hacked off. A quick pace was recommended, and indeed decreed, as we went along this street.

On that very first visit to the shopping centre we stayed for some time then decided we might as well walk home. We made two mistakes. Firstly we underestimated the distance and time it would take and secondly we had not yet realised how suddenly, so much further south than the UK, the sun dropped steeply below the horizon. By the time we got back it was nearly dark, which was a bit alarming in view of reports circulating about the dangers, and we were once again out too late with our shorts on.

Going out on excursions did break the monotony but there were quite a number of good facilities on camp. There was a row of shops, with native occupants. One was an excellent bookshop, from which I bought new hardbacks regularly. I knocked up a small bookcase from scrap timber and created a small library, making parcels up as the collection outgrew this and posting them home in batches. There was a café piled high with Coca-Cola and other refreshing drinks, a fruit stall and a barber's shop. Here you could get a short-back-and-sides in about three minutes flat and also a shave, which some brave chaps underwent as the barber jabbered away excitedly in a mixture of Arabic and fractured English while waving his arms all around their faces brandishing an open cut-throat razor.

The currency we used was Egyptian piastres, or 'ackers' as we called them, for some reason, with one hundred to the pound. The paper money covered all but the very lowest denominations, which came in coins of assorted strange shapes, including some much-worn ones that looked like washers, with a hole in the middle. This money circulated almost exclusively around the areas frequented by service people and rarely saw a bank. Consequently the notes, especially the smaller ones, rapidly became dirty and worn. Sometimes you had to persuade a trader that the dog-eared piece of paper offered, so worn that you could hardly read the printing and held together with bits of sticky paper, was legal tender. The NAAFI issued red and green plastic discs as five and ten piastre tokens for use in their own establishments although they were accepted widely throughout the area of military occupation.

Just past the shops was the YMCA, a pleasant building with a walled courtyard, all built in the ubiquitous sandstone and which we soon found was a much nicer place to pass an hour or two than the NAAFI. The main hall was an excellent cafeteria and off it was a shop selling not only such necessities as dusters, soap, polish and razor blades but also a range of silks, rugs, gifts and carved mementos for posting home. A wing to one side contained a billiard table where I played some inexpert games of snooker, so long as someone would constantly tell me the values of the balls.

The matching wing across the courtyard was set aside for evening record recitals. One of the airmen would introduce and play music over a loudspeaker from an adjoining cubicle. I developed an interest in traditional jazz which was a regular feature, becoming familiar with the earlier players such as Jelly Roll Morton, Bix Beiderbecke and, of course, old Satchmo, as well as the up and coming British exponents who were keeping this art form alive, like Humphrey Lyttelton and Chris Barber.

The Astra Cinema was also a sandstone structure offering a change of programme twice a week and screening all the most up-to-date American releases, sometimes before they reached the West End of London. I recall being impressed by two particularly stunning films; 'Seven Brides for Seven Brothers' and Hitchcock's 'Rear Window'.

The cinema was also the venue for any show-business celebrities who from time to time toured round the overseas military zones. Harry Secombe came and, unlike some, who only mixed with the officers, afterwards insisted on finding the airmen's NAAFI, where he played a cod game of darts with the boys. 'Two-Ton' Tessie O'Shea entertained us and the next day was seen on top of a photographer's indignant camel in Fayid shopping centre. Terry-Thomas was a great success. In those days he was doing a sketch about a disc-jockey who had accidentally broken all his records. This obliged him to perform them all himself, providing him with an opportunity to display his considerable powers of imper-sonation.

Not all artistes met with universal approval, however. I looked forward to seeing and hearing Turner Layton, being familiar from the radio with the beautiful voice of this very distinguished singer who had, before the war, been one half of the best and most famous of all the duettist acts, Layton and Johnstone. He embarked on his programme of baritone ballads but after several of these the audience grew restless. This sort of thing was not to their taste, especially from a black man, and to my disgust the reaction became so hostile that he was obliged to abandon his act. 'Cheerful Charlie Chester' didn't even get as far as our camp, although ex-pected. The story was that at his first engagement he had bounded onto the stage saying "Hi boys! I bet you lot can't wait to trade in your buckets and spades and do some real soldiering!" – for which he had been booed off the stage and went home, presumably less cheerful.

The washing and sanitary arrangements, particularly for the tented site, were less than luxurious. There was a shack, open to the elements at the top and bottom, containing benches with a number of rather unsavoury galvanised basins for washing, the water being supplied through taps sprouting from a pipe running along the line. An area with sprinklers overhead served for showers. All the water was cold, or at least not heated, which made for an uncomfortable shave. It was drawn initially from the Sweet Water Canal, then passed through a filtration plant and, with chemicals added, was distributed as fit for use. Its supply was a bit unpredictable and one day dried up completely, leaving some of us covered in soap, which we towelled off as well as we could. The reason for this stoppage was widely believed to have been a blockage caused by one of the dead donkeys that occasionally added fragrance to the source of the water. The same bitter water, distributed for drinking by tanker lorries, was decanted into large earthenware pots sitting in wooden frames about the place.

A visit to the toilet block was less than a delight, especially if you were squeamish or easily embarrassed. Another long structure, open to the sky, contained a row of cubicles with wooden seats, each pierced with a round hole, set over a large bucket. The hessian sides of these cubicles projected only about two feet, with no doors, so the seated occupants would conduct conversations with their neighbours while passers-by had a full view of their exertions. Not much fun for anyone when the occasional diarrhoea was being suffered! Extra buckets for urinating stood at each end of the block. All these buckets contained a thick, foul-smelling layer of disinfectant, which in theory floated to the top of the con-tents and deterred the flies. They were emptied on a regular basis by a team of Arab labourers into a bowser like a petrol lorry, which then left the camp for remote disposal. The buckets under the cubicle seats were removed from outside through trapdoors at the back and it was possible to be seated not above a bucket but a pair of groping brown hands.

There was consternation on one occasion when a case of typhoid was suspected. The whole camp had to be tested as a precaution and we all queued up at the medical office to be handed a small bottle and a cardboard cup with a lid, in order that samples could be submitted, a process that had to be repeated over three consecutive mornings. Daily we would return our samples, the bottles going onto a shelf with others in all shades of brown, green and yellow, and clear or frothy, depending on one's favourite tipple. The liquids presented no problem, but the trouble with the solids was that many of us developed constipation, possibly through the need to perform three days in a row and having to do so publicly. As the three days had to be uninterrupted it was in some cases a long time before all the testing was concluded, after which it transpired that the original case was a false alarm!

After a morning's 'work', a mid-day meal and a shower, more often than not the afternoon would be spent lounging on our beds, which were usually dragged out into the scorching sunshine. We were supposed to protect our eyes with the sunglasses that had been issued as part of our tropical kit but no-one dared to be the first sissy to put them on. The heat helped to kill the bedbugs. These had a habit of crawling on you, burying their heads under your skin and sucking up your blood. If noticed, an automatic brush off with the hand would merely leave a decapitated head in your body; a favourite way to make them withdraw was to touch them with a lighted cigarette. They lived behind the buttons of mattresses and in the tightly-coiled bed springs and were quite impervious to the thick powder that was issued for their eradication. We would lie there contemplating our drab surroundings, all in various shades of khaki. Our clothes were khaki and our skins were turning khaki. The sand was, as were the tents around us, all buildings within sight and any passing vehicles.

The Egyptian fly is a clever chap. He never moves fast, constantly landing on sticky face, arm or any bare skin. Nevertheless, however suddenly and quickly you might strike, he rarely gets flattened, lazily moving out of the way and coming straight back. Most of us had a personal fly-swatter, some decoratively fashioned in the workshop, and could eventually line up a small row of corpses of the few that weren't quite quick enough. Many of us worked on our tans, gradually uncovering more of the white parts judiciously. One keen sun-worshipper persevered with this over a period, removing increasingly more articles of clothing including his underwear, until with some pride he could say that only one small part of his body was un-tanned and that he covered with a small flannel when he was stretched out in the sun. Unfortunately he fell asleep and a 'mate' removed the flannel. He was later carted off to the Medical Officer in agony.

One afternoon, as we idly watched the approach of the tanker that took away the waste from the toilet block, someone said, "It'll be worth watching the shit-wagon today."

"Why?"

"Just watch, that's all."

It was always an entertaining spectacle. A dozen or so Arabs in disgusting overalls would jump off the lorry and form a human chain to the toilet block, jabbering away excitedly in Arabic and with much gesticulation. The large buckets, which stood about two feet tall, would be passed along until one of the workers, having drawn the short straw, would heave them up in the air for the man on top to grab and empty into the tank through the round hatch. Frequently the buckets were full to capacity and the man doing the lifting would struggle to keep them upright, quite regularly spilling some of the contents down his chest. The much polluted site where all this took place was an area of sand to be avoided.

I was surprised that we weren't always contracting unpleasant diseases but with the exception of the false alarm over typhoid very rarely was anyone the subject of any medical concern, due presumably to the cocktail of drugs we had all received.

On this occasion things seemed even more difficult than usual and one bucket caused each link in the chain to shout and wave his arms about greatly. The lifter got it up with the greatest difficulty and much spillage and the man on top tipped it towards the hatch gingerly. As it reached the horizontal there was a great rumbling noise and something heavy rolled out and dropped in the tanker. He bent over to peer inside and with a great splash a jet of the foul contents shot back up and hit him squarely in the face.

"Blimey! What was that?" one of us asked.

"A shot... as in shot-put . I nicked it from the gym."

Simple minds are easily tickled, especially when there's little other amusement.

One afternoon our peace was disturbed by the sight and sound of something resembling a model helicopter. It may have been a hornet but whatever, it had a body like a sausage, a wingspan of at least eight inches and looked extremely angry and dangerous. It dived into the tent. Eventually it reappeared and flew off, only to return shortly afterwards. We tried to see where it was going which was somewhere near the back corner of the tent. It went away again and we searched our living quarters. Between the back of the wooden side wall and the sand we discovered a white conical construction. It was building a nest; we would soon be infested by a whole family of them! Gingerly we destroyed the nest and disposed of it. On the next visitation the creature searched about for a bit and finally departed for good.

Instead of a morning Billet Orderly we had a Site Orderly. The occupants of each tent were responsible for the condition of their own quarters and the Site Orderly checked the site for any waste paper or obvious untidiness. On my turn I did all that then smartened myself up for inspection. Finally, in accordance with our normal procedure, I dragged a broom in ever-increasing circles round the tent to create a pristine area of sand. There was no way of getting back into the tent without disturbing the effect of this so I hid the broom somewhere and awaited the visit of the Orderly Officer.

"Site ready for your inspection, sir."

He took one look at me.

"Sergeant, take his name; he's got dirty boots."

And he moved on.

"Excuse me sir, but I have dust on them because I've been all over the place, checking the site."

There was no answer and, for the only time in my four years, I found myself officially on a charge – for having dusty boots in the desert! They didn't call it that; it was something about 'conduct prejudicial to good order and in contravention of Queen's Regulations'. So I found myself being marched in front of a senior officer with my hat off. The sergeant read out the charge against me, concluding with the words "while on active service". The officer ignored my attempted defence and 'awarded' me seven days jankers. There was, of course, no way of appealing against injustices.

"Are we on active service, sarge?" I asked in surprise as we came out.

"Yes, officially."

"What does that mean?"

"Only one thing out here. Your sentence is automatically increased. Normally you would have got only three days."

So for a week I trudged back and forth to the guardroom, bulled up in full kit, numerous times each day to be very critically inspected by the RAF Police. In my 'spare time' I had to report to the mess for kitchen duties.

An all too frequent interruption to an otherwise mostly uneventful existence was the necessity of guard duty, which was a serious business, not without dangers. The native workers had to leave the premises by nightfall but they, or others, would occasionally break in later and steal cigarettes, drink or anything else worth having from the NAAFI or elsewhere. They were incredibly cunning and adept at this, rarely being caught, in spite of our considerable precautions and vigilance. Several possibly apocryphal stories circulated. The occupants of one tent were supposed to have woken up one day in the open air, their tent having been stolen in the night! Another tale concerned an Air Force motorbike belonging to the Motor Transport Section. This section had an area of sand surrounded by garages that had been watered and rolled repeatedly and hardened by the sun to make a yard almost as firm as concrete for the vehicles. With an inventory of all stock due, the transport people had discovered to their embarrassment that they possessed one motorcycle more than could be accounted for in the paperwork, so they wrapped one carefully in protective sheeting and buried it in the yard, flattening the surface again. When they dug for it several days later, it wasn't there! During this time the yard had been patrolled regularly and was flood-lit all night.

What I can vouch for is the fact that one night a guard reported a hole in the perimeter fence, another was spotted later on at a different place and in the morning the NAAFI reported the loss of several thousand cigarettes. Throughout this time the perimeter fence was patrolled, with small searchlights sweeping the desert at intervals and extra guards were posted at vulnerable sites like the NAAFI. Then one night, as we looked out across the intervening bit of desert to the perimeter lights of RAF Fayid nearby, they all went out and stayed out. In the morning we learned that hundreds of metres of valuable power cable buried under the ground had completely disappeared. Things had been known to vanish from the mess without the camp's defences actually being breached. Tins of food were almost certainly passed to the labourers on the toilet wagon, who dropped them inside their fetid tank, to be retrieved later on outside the camp.

Guard duty covered the twelve hours from six pm to six am and, at certain sensitive sites, the full 24 hours, all undertaken in shifts, with two hours 'on' and four hours 'off' in rotation. The entire boundary was patrolled in modest beats, with the NAAFI and the station's own electricity generating station being among extra locations. All this resulted in a large contingent every night being on duty, which therefore came round less than every fortnight. During the winter it got very cold indeed at night. Not only were we grateful for the thicker blue uniforms worn at this time of year but at night we put on pyjamas under them and greatcoats over them.

Having been listed for duty, we reported at the armoury to draw a rifle and some rounds of ammunition, then fell in on the parade ground to form the official party to celebrate the daily lowering of the Royal Air Force flag, which was accompanied by a rendition of the Last Post. Duty Buglers were excused other duties, so volunteers abounded, with or without much musical talent, and it was difficult to keep a straight face at such a solemn occasion as some of them struggled to produce a recognisable version. We then marched to the guardroom to be allocated our patrols.

Regularly during the shift you marched back and forth, sometimes meeting your neighbour at the turn-round point, and occasionally stopped to sweep the terrain outside the wire fence with a small searchlight mounted on a tower. Time dragged, particularly on a late shift in the small hours. I used to force myself not to look at my watch, counting seconds in my head to estimate the passing of another ten minutes. The time elapsed usually turned out to be about three minutes.

The biggest problem was how to address the Orderly Officer, who plodded round the entire place at some time during the night to see if there was anything to report or, I suppose, to see if you were still awake. They were all different. Standing instructions were to challenge all comers with "Halt! Who goes there?" followed, if appropriate, with "Place your identification on the ground and retreat." You then inspected this (in the dark!) and allowed the visitor to advance. If you did this to the Orderly Officer he was likely to explode with impatience and say "You can see perfectly well who I am" and give you a severe telling off. If, on the other hand, you recognised an officer approaching, from inside the wire of course, and said "Good evening, sir", you had probably picked one of those who expected the full protocol, who would say "But for all you know I am an Arab in disguise" and threaten to put you on a charge.

One night, while staring out into the darkness across the sand, I thought I picked out something white in the distance, moving slightly among the shallow dunes. The next time it appeared to have moved a bit nearer. I didn't see how it could be anything other than an Arab in his white jellaba, stealing gradually further forward on his stomach. With some apprehension I cocked my rifle and prepared to challenge when a final light breeze brought the object right up to the fence.

It was a piece of newspaper.

During the off-shift periods we could slip away to the NAAFI or YMCA in the evening but during the night we dossed down, fully-dressed, on bunks in the guardroom. Sleep was virtually impossible and the four-hour break would be interrupted half-way through by others changing shifts. On one occasion, in the dead of night, the whole off-shift guard was roused and turned out for an emergency. A large theft had occurred and the perpetrators were believed to be making off across the desert. Some of us jumped onto lorries, which shot off over the sand.

"Put one up the spout and release the safety catch," the sergeant ordered. For the first and thankfully the last time I considered the real possibility that I might be ordered to shoot somebody. We never found anyone.

The small lamps around the wire were very feeble but at one point near the rear of the camp stood a real 90 centimetre searchlight and we electricians were frequently appointed to the patrol where it was. The first task each evening was to start up its large diesel generator, which stood on the back of a lorry. This took some doing, as you opened up valves and struggled to get enough momentum going with the starting handle, before slamming the valves closed again. All this customarily took a number of attempts. At intervals, when you wanted to use the light, you set the two carbons close together, switched on and flinched from the small explosion of the resulting arc, then pulled the carbons apart until maximum illumination was obtained. This powerful beam could light up everything in its path, even the slopes of the small hill some distance away. The movements were controlled at the end of a long arm by a wheel over a semi-circular trench worn by constant use. Strict instructions were issued to keep the beam at ground level, as someone had recently trained it on a plane landing at RAF Fayid, blinding the pilot, who had been obliged to circle until a message had been relayed to the guard.

One of the sites requiring 24-hour cover was a large gap in the fence on the side facing the airfield next door, filled with half a dozen portable barriers covered in barbed wire. This duty fell to me only once, thankfully. The time dragged interminably throughout the four cycles of on and off periods, day and night. In mid-afternoon I watched a large aeroplane approaching across the space between the two camps. To my consternation it taxied right up to me. The pilot, who I could see was a commissioned officer, shouted and gesticulated at me. I approached, saluted and challenged him. I had no instructions about this sort of thing. He waved his arms some more and, over the noise of the engines, mouthed a request to be admitted. I hesitated.

"Open the damn gate when you're ordered!" he yelled.

I quite easily lip-read what he said and yanked sections of the barrier out of the way. The aircraft duly came through and made its way to a hangar for some sort of maintenance. As with the Derbyshire sheep, I wished I had been fore-warned.

One of the snags about the recurrent spells of guard duty was the danger of omitting to turn up for them, with the inevitable consequence of being put on a charge. It was absolutely essential to scan the official noticeboard on a daily basis to see whether you were detailed for duties, this being the only source of such information. This board also notified all other important facts, such as examination results and carried a regular Situation Report or SITREP. This document informed us of all noteworthy incidents throughout the zone. From it we learned, at different times, that a civilian cinema manager had been attacked and badly injured in the theft of his evening's takings, that motorcycle dispatch riders after dark should know that wires had been seen stretched across roads to bring them down (also for what cash could be had) and that three soldiers, somewhere in the zone, had suffocated after being set to dig a deep trench in the sand as a punishment.

The food at Abyad, under what must have been difficult conditions, was surprisingly good. My particular favourites were the salads. Cold meats could be accompanied by as much raw lettuce, carrots, onions and chopped white cabbage as you wanted, which was appreciated in the heat of summer. This didn't please the vociferous minority, who demanded and got us less of this 'rabbit food' and more good old British hot stodge, in temperatures of a hundred degrees or more.

The privilege of leave was a mixed blessing. Although still amounting to thirty days a year, there was normally nowhere to spend them. You still made the three daily visits to the mess, and lounged about in the mornings as well as the afternoons, explaining to any Orderly Officer or Sergeant why you were not at work.

Over the Christmas period the workshops closed and all but a few on important duties took a week's break, celebrating in as festive a mood as possible. Decorations were put up in tents and huts and little parties were organised. Hardly anyone went to the mess, apart from Christmas Day, when a real Christmas dinner was laid on, which, in keeping with Air Force tradition, the lower ranks had served to them at tables by the officers. Parcels from home contained cakes, Christmas puddings, tinned meat and other goodies. The manageress of the YMCA agreed to cook a certain number of undernourished chickens, which the native bearers got for us at a price. With these, some fruit and other bits and pieces, along with a good supply of alcohol, we could make some sort of feast in the tent that lasted several days. All this food in our accommodation was strictly contrary to the regulations, as was the greatly increased use of clandestine electrical equipment to heat puddings and soup or brew tea and coffee. All we were short of was bread, so we made a cautious excursion to the airmen's mess to see if we could scrounge any, where we banged straight into the Catering Officer and desperately tried to think up an excuse for being in the kitchen. We were surprised to be greeted with a cheerful, "Hello, chaps! Do you want anything? Bread, butter, potatoes? You might as well have it; no-one's coming here and it'll only get thrown away."

While I was in Egypt I clocked up two birthdays, my twenty-first and twenty-second, with an attempt at some sort of celebration. Some four months after my twenty-first I received a card from the Electoral Registration Officer at Hertford to say that I was now eligible as a service voter and he had appointed my father as proxy.

There was one very enjoyable way in which one leave a year might be spent and that was a holiday in Cyprus, a very great centre for British troops in those days. If you made your own arrangements for accommodation or stayed at one of the services holiday centres, the Royal Air Force was prepared to fly a certain number over there, a distance of only about three hundred miles, free of charge.

I put my name down and went – twice.

8. On Leave in Cyprus

With a friend, Gordon from Bromsgrove, I had a flight to Cyprus reserved and we had booked for a fortnight in a hotel in Famagusta, by post. Some time before this became due we were unexpectedly offered the chance of an extra immediate weekend break on the island. This was a considerable surprise, as places on these trips, available throughout the entire Air Force presence in the Zone, were booked in advance and hard to come by, making some use of the unoccupied seats on regular training flights of various aircraft.

With notification coming only on the morning of the Friday we were to go, we grabbed a few clothes and belongings and reported to the Air Movements section at RAF Fayid. Here we passed through Customs, Quarantine and Currency Exchange and, after several delays for some technical reason, took off in a Valetta aircraft bound for Nicosia airport. We teamed up with three other chaps, one of whom had been recommended a small hotel in Nicosia, though whether we would all be able to find rooms was uncertain. Upon landing and before we were let out, someone came round and squirted a disinfectant gun over us. Cyprus was not to be infected by anything unsavoury arriving from the land of the Pharaohs.

The five of us grabbed a taxi, which careered off in the direction of central Nicosia, with us speculating on the rule of the road, left or right; it appeared to be straight down the middle. In fact, officially, they drove on the left. As with many facilities, such as phone kiosks, pillar boxes and street signs, things were done the British way, Cyprus being under British rule at that time, well before the split into two countries with a demarcation line of barbed wire fencing separating them. There were Greeks, Turks and a few Arabs, all seeming to get on well, and vast numbers of British Army and Air Force personnel stationed in the many camps.

We arrived unannounced in the evening at the Ver de Luna Hotel on the northern side of the city. This attractive single-storey place had only five bedrooms but the pleasant lady owner welcomed us and, with the addition of three extra beds in a small twin room, all butted up to each other, squeezed us in. After an excellent dinner we wandered into town. In Metaxas Square we were accosted by taxi drivers.

"Hey, you want a good time? I take you to see my sister; very pretty, very clean and only sixteen." Their 'sisters' were always 'sixteen'. We passed on and entered one of the night-clubs or cabarets that we had heard about. It seemed very quiet. Sitting at a lonely table we ordered drinks. My Coca-Cola was the outrageous price of two shillings (well, it was outrageous then; a whole bottle of the local *Commandaria* wine was available in shops for just four shillings). There was no entertainment and we returned to our hotel, having another drink at the attractive little bar. This was presided over by a charming and talkative Russian lady who told us, among other things, that she had a cat called 'Pushkin'. She listened to our complaints and told us where we had gone wrong in our innocence. These places charged a lot for the first drink only, in lieu of an entrance fee, and expected to sell something more profitable than Coca-Cola. Also, we had gone in too early, the cabaret didn't start until at least midnight. We felt stupid but none of us had ever been on a foreign holiday before, or even to a British nightclub.

As we started to get ready for bed one of my new ac-quaintances said, "I'm going back to the square to get a taxi driver to take me to a girl."

"You're not serious! She won't be sixteen nor, perhaps, very clean."

"Maybe, but I've been promising myself a bit after over a year away from home and she'll be a great improvement on the bints back in Egypt."

That was true. The 'bints' in our part of Egypt, apart from the rare WRAF or NAAFI girl, were women in the local village, who were dirty and, being covered from head to toe in black garments, of indeterminate vintage, not to mention 'out of bounds'. Most Cypriot girls, on the other hand, were very pretty. He returned some time later, somewhat the worse for wear.

"How did you get on? Did you go to a knocking-shop or a private house?"

He groaned. "Neither. I had to sit in the back of his taxi until he had got two more customers; then we drove to somewhere in the backstreets and parked on a piece of waste ground. He beeped his horn three times and three women came out of a house and got into the back of the taxi. We did it all in there ... together."

"What was yours like?"

"I can't be certain. First of all it was pitch black, then there were arms and legs all over the place. I'm not even sure that the one I was kissing was the one that I was having!"

"You'll have to go for tests when you get back."

"Yes, I expect so. I believe you have to wait some time before you are pronounced OK."

"Did you enjoy it?"

"No!"

Waking up in the morning in Cyprus was a real pleasure. Outside were unfamiliar noises: the sound of birdsong mingling with normal civilian activities; people getting into cars, greeting each other and sweeping their patios. The daylight scene showed us a country still a bit arid but much greener than we had seen since leaving the UK, with flowers and foliage decorating the balconies and porches of the houses.

After a full breakfast we set off to take a proper look at Nicosia, doing something that wasn't possible after the division of the city in 1974; we walked right round the top of the completely circular sixteenth century Venetian walls, pierced in a few places for modern roads. We admired the architecture, notably the thirteenth century Saint Sophia mosque, with its twin minarets rising incongruously atop a gothic cathedral, and explored markets and shops. In a music shop I asked for a record of typical Cypriot singing and bought one labelled in Greek. With great care I managed to get this breakable '78' back to Egypt and later on, packed in foam in a parcel, had it sent home. I've still got it and I still don't know what it's all about.

After lunch the hotel proprietor kindly phoned for a taxi to enable us to explore further. For a very modest fare the driver took us out for a whole afternoon, acting as a guide to all the places of interest. Off the road to Kyrenia we climbed a narrow track with hairpin bends to St Hilarion Castle, perched on the ridge of the northern mountain range, then down again and across to the beautiful Bellapais Abbey. This well-preserved thirteenth century church with its cloister was still used by the villagers. In the forecourt stood a tree producing both oranges and lemons, a result of clever grafting. Finally we went down to Kyrenia, with its fortress and pretty harbour, then it was back to the hotel.

After dinner our intention was to go to a cinema showing one of the new wide-screen films, followed by a more informed visit to a cabaret. As a result of two action-packed days, however, and a substantial meal, we all actually fell asleep on our beds, not waking until well after midnight. We were too tired to bother.

On the Sunday another taxi took us the forty miles across to Famagusta, with its old harbour and walls. Another orthodox cathedral had been converted to a mosque by the unusual-looking addition of a minaret. Inside, on the areas around the edges of the great carpet, were the shoes and sandals of the faithful. Coffee was then taken at the wide beach in the suburb of Varosha, then boasting only two hotels. We sat on the terrace of the Florida Hotel, which was where Gordon and I would be staying on our forthcoming two-week stay, and very nice it seemed. A dash back to Nicosia was followed by another taxi ride to the airport and an arrival back at our dear little tent late in the evening. The entire weekend had involved the expenditure of no more than £5 each! I said so in the letter I sent home about the trip, so it must have been true.

In due course, Gordon and I went back on our long-planned two-week holiday, this time with proper preparation, including applying in advance to the Cypriot authorities for temporary driving licences, as we proposed to hire a motorcycle, although unfortunately these hadn't arrived. Even with advance arrangements and a firm hotel booking there was a certain amount of confusion and our flight, in a Viking of Eagle Airways Ltd, was suddenly brought forward by twenty-four hours and we had to rise at 4.45 am. Arriving in Nicosia in mid-morning, we managed to get booked into the Ver de Luna again for one night. After one of their excellent lunches we went into town and sought out one of the many firms renting out motorcycles. First we explained the problem over our driving licences and for a sum of money the proprietor agreed to get the necessary forms and stamps for us. We picked a 500cc BSA Star, about seven years old and somewhat battered, tried it out round the block, and booked it for the fortnight.

Then we wandered about the old narrow streets of Nicosia, with workshops producing pottery, copper vases, leather harnesses and furniture. There were no greengrocers' shops, all fruit and vegetables being obtained from the large covered market, where we bought some apples at two shillings an 'ock'. We handled some weights and bought half an ock, which felt like about two pounds. Climbing the narrow spiral steps of one of St Sophia's minarets gave us a splendid view of the whole city and surrounding plain. After dinner we went to the cinema, one of the outdoor places that were so much more comfortable in summer, to see 'The Devil Makes Three', an unusual non-musical Gene Kelly film, also starring Pier Angeli and set in post-war Europe. Greek subtitles were projected onto a separate screen. Twice during the main feature an unnatural interval was introduced and the lights put on for the sale of Coca-Cola.

In the morning the motorcycle man arrived in a taxi to take us to the Traffic Branch, where we handed over mug-shots that we had had the foresight to bring with us. These were affixed to temporary driving licences and we were now legal. Collecting our bike, we were now mobile and had a wider look round the capital.

After a first-rate lunch we set out for Famagusta, forty miles away on the east coast. As we did not want to change back out of our civilian clothes, we stuffed everything else into our luggage, which consisted of my suitcase and Gordon's large and small packs, with the exception of our awkward peaked caps, which the hotel allowed us to leave until our return. We arranged ourselves on the bike, with Gordon wearing the small pack on his chest, me behind wearing the large pack on my back and the suitcase wedged between us, and set off, stopping twice for a break and to change drivers.

We thought, at the time, that the Florida Hotel was wonderful. Retrospectively it did not compare entirely with modern establishments. The guests were mostly British, many of them servicemen on leave, and included a couple of beautiful air-hostesses, far too snooty to associate with the common lower ranks. For some reason the manager had to put us in a temporary bedroom for two days. This had no washbasin and a full-length window with no curtains, immediately over the front door. This meant we had to undress in the dark, especially as it was so hot that we slept naked.

The chambermaid was a cheerful dumpy woman with about three words of English. 'Tonight' meant shortly, 'press' was something you did to trousers and 'finish' was an all-purpose conclusion to a conversation. Nevertheless, she would treat us to a rambling anecdote in Greek every day. On the third morning she beckoned us to follow her, no doubt to our permanent room. She knocked on a door and as it opened to reveal the air-hostesses she said, "Alright tonight?"

With great disdain, the girls flounced off.

In our new quarters we gained a washbasin and lost a window. The room had been formed by sub-dividing a larger one and the light came through a high glazed panel via the outer bedroom. Standing on a chair you could actually see from one room into the other!

Meals were excellent and the times flexible, packed lunches being provided if required. The head waiter, a most helpful individual, would knock at the bedroom door to remind you if you were late for breakfast. When you came down he would rattle off in moderately good English, but delivered like a machine gun, all in one word, "boilegg-scrambleeggfryeggbaconomelettecheeseyoulikecoffee?" One of the specialities at dinner was red mullet. It was the first time I had looked at food that looked back.

The manager, a pleasant man, had a beautiful younger sister helping him. One of the Air Force guests tried to photograph her every time she appeared. Each time she evaded him and dodged away. Assuming this to be natural shyness, he finally pursued her into the kitchen, where he received the full wrath of the outraged manager. When the manager calmed down he explained that nice Cypriot girls would not allow themselves to be photographed alone by strangers; it was against moral custom. Children and workers in the countryside showed no such reluctance and it was sometimes difficult to snap a local scene without a line of grinning faces in the foreground. No doubt the different cultures had different rules although we found it difficult to know Greeks from Turks as they were so integrated.

Three miles up the road from the Florida was a services leave camp, one of several on the island. We could have stayed there, under military administration, but as it was permitted to use respectable hotels we had much preferred to do this. The Golden Sands Camp was useful to us, though, as clothes could be laundered there free of charge.

Once we were settled in to our new surroundings we turned our attention to some serious sightseeing. We soon discovered that the tyres on the motorbike were worn smooth, as were those on all other rented machines. This was not to be unexpected if all hirers covered the distances on rough roads that we did; in the two weeks we clocked up 2,000 miles! In old Famagusta we climbed the massive ancient walls to look over the harbour and the town. Although there was a thriving population there were many houses and churches in a state of ruin, apparently their stone having been taken and shipped over to Egypt to line the Suez Canal when it was being constructed.

The first planned long trip was past Salamis, the 'Pompeii' of Cyprus and one-time capital, across the northern mountain range then all the way along the coast to Kyrenia, a total distance that appeared eighty miles or so according to the rudimentary map available. Some of the mountain roads doubled back on themselves constantly and along the coast the numerous rocky inlets necessitated many inland detours, adding considerably to the mileage. Much of the route ran over poor surfaces and a low gear was frequently necessary. Miles from anywhere, and far short of Kyrenia, we ran out of petrol with over 150 miles registered on the clock.

On the beach were several parked cars but no-one could help. The first vehicle to come along after a considerable wait was a lorry with a load of gravel. We waved and in sign language explained our predicament to the two occupants. Between us we tried and failed to get the bike up onto the lorry but the men indicated that they would take me into Kyrenia for fuel while Gordon guarded the bike. There was not really room for a third passenger in the cab but with my legs crossed and body turned sideways they managed to slam the door on me. On the outskirts of town, after some miles, they dropped me off at a filling station, literally, because my cramped legs had seized up with severe pins and needles and I fell in a heap on the verge.

The garage owner didn't understand how pins and needles had got into me but he picked me up and sold me a can of petrol. In reasonable English he suggested that by far the quickest and cheapest way to return was on the back of his friend's motorcycle, so I paid for that. The friend had little English but had instructions that after about ten miles I would tap him on the shoulder. Some two hundred yards down the road we passed Gordon on our bike, belting into town in the opposite direction. I nudged my driver and asked him to stop.

"OK Ten miles," he said, and kept going, until I finally got him to turn round, somewhat mystified.

Gordon was waiting for me; only ten minutes after I had left him a lorry had stopped and siphoned a gallon of fuel off for him. We filled up completely and, after a cursory look at Kyrenia, drove on the seventeen miles to Nicosia. It was now dark and, availing ourselves once more of the hospitable Ver de Luna, we had a late dinner then drove the forty miles back to our hotel.

Most of the next day was spent relaxing on the beach and swimming in the clear blue Mediterranean, so much more pleasant than the excessive saltiness of the Great Bitter Lake, and after dinner we went to the pictures in Nicosia, another eighty mile round trip. The film, 'The Robe', was to start at 10.30 pm, the cinema being another outdoor affair. Well before the gates to the compound opened, a large crowd assembled, with much pushing and demanding to be admitted, some climbing up on the high walls and haranguing the attendants. All this increased with time until, in some alarm, we were lifted off our feet in the crush and pushed backwards and forwards.

Eventually we were let in to watch the wonderful new invention called 'Cinemascope'. I was disappointed. The wraparound sound was impressive but the picture was not the '3D' suggested by the advertising, merely wide. The film, a European version, had various foreign subtitles. Supplementary projectors showed translations on screens at both sides and along the top in Greek, Turkish and Arabic. Only one member of the family behind us could read and he loudly interpreted the whole thing for the others.

On the way home we were stopped by the military police and required to show our 1250's, although not in uniform, as apparently a couple of soldiers had gone Absent Without Leave. It was after three when we fell into bed.

Next afternoon we set off again, through Larnaca and to Lefkara, where the women sat out in the sun, making the famous local lace. We were dragged into a house to be sold some and invited to explore the village, where a football match was taking place, in August, on a dusty pitch without a single blade of grass. Because of the British presence almost everybody not only spoke English but had either been to England or would be going shortly. It was common to be addressed "Hello, Johnny! Do you come from Bristol?" or "I was in Blackpool two months ago."

On the way out in the mornings on these trips we would pass through the main thoroughfares of towns and villages. In the evenings detours were often necessary, chairs being placed at both ends of the principal street to form a pedestrian area. This is where the serious 'courting' took place, the young men and women, in the strict company of their parents, walking to and fro and assessing each other from a chaste distance. It all seemed very old-fashioned, as was the agriculture. Rudimentary farm equipment was towed behind the various animals and threshing was accomplished by dragging a flint-studded board over the fields, weighed down by the grandmother sitting on a chair on top.

Needless to say, we enjoyed nothing but brilliant sunny weather the whole time, very hot at the coast and a bit cooler in the main Troodos Mountains. On our trip into this beautiful wooded area we climbed through valleys and ravines, stopping at the delightful town of Platres, where an elderly gentleman took an interest in our photographic equipment and invited us into his garden for the best views across the valley. He had a stereoscopic viewer and showed us three-dimensional pictures of the area that he had taken fifty years earlier, at the beginning of the twentieth century. We were also offered a glass of water straight from a spring, which was sparklingly clear and refreshingly cold.

Wherever we stopped for a Coca-Cola, either in towns or at remote wayside kiosks, it was always served chilled and with ice, and tea and coffee always came with a glass of cold water. Pushing on, passing near Pine Tree Camp, another services leave centre, we stopped at the summit of Mount Olympus, from where a view of the whole country could be enjoyed.

Taking a different road back, towards Nicosia, we passed through an area where asbestos was being mined. Its white dust lay across the road and surroundings! A loaded lorry came round the corner, the driver inevitably stopping and jumping out to have his photograph taken. He handed us each a lump of grey ore with a narrow seam of asbestos running through it as a souvenir. I kept mine for some years until the dangers of this substance were realised.

The next afternoon we ran out of petrol again, still not appreciating the difference between an apparent straight line on the map and its actual course on the roads. With the small contents of the reserve tank we coasted to the next village where one of a group of curious youngsters climbed onto the pillion and directed me to a house in the back streets, while Gordon sat on a wall in the fast fading evening light. A villager sold me a gallon from a rusty tin at twice the filling-station price and we pushed on, only to find that the engine was running rough, which we attributed to dirty fuel. We proceeded in fits and starts then the lights suddenly failed. In the illumination of a cottage window we realised that the battery lead had become disconnected and fixed it back on as best as we could, the machine not being equipped with any tools. Next day we coaxed the bike to a garage where the fuel and float chamber were pronounced clean but the sparking plug was found to have virtually no points left. After attention and expense we were back in running order.

But it wasn't long before that neglected machine was again giving us a headache. The day of our long excursion right round the island did not exactly work to plan, to say the least. Our proposed route would take us through Larnaca, Limassol, Paphos, Xeron, Morphou and Nicosia but after only twenty miles the front tyre suddenly deflated. We pushed the bike back to the last village, where we were taken to a man 'who knew about these things'. He removed the wheel, took off the tyre and we discovered that the valve had completely parted company from the inner tube, which in itself looked fairly good, with no patches. After financial negotiation he took Gordon and the tube on his pillion to somewhere where it could be repaired, no new one being available. They were gone well over two hours. Apparently the vulcanising was done by steam in a small workshop, a protracted operation compared to modern methods.

After enjoying our packed lunch on the seashore, we pushed on. But before long, the rear tyre also collapsed! With difficulty we ran the bike in first gear and walked beside it the four miles into Larnaca to find a garage. The tube was a mass of patches and signs of perishing, while the tyre was not only paper thin but showing evidence of cracking round the sides. This time a complete new tyre and tube were in stock, which set us back a further considerable sum of money.

While we were waiting for all this to be done, a man on a tricycle selling drink of some sort stopped outside. We had seen a number of these things on our travels and wondered what was on offer. A huge glass jar contained a white liquid, which was ladled into tumblers and mixed with various spices from assorted containers that hung round the tricycle. The drink was obviously appreciated by the local population.

"Hello, British boys. Want a nice drink?"

"What is it?"

He attempted to explain in fractured English and we understood that it was *beestings* – the first milk from a goat after giving birth.

"I give you some for free," he said, and ladled some out, sprinkling it from his collection of herbs and powders. Gordon and I sipped it and looked at each other. It was, without exception, the most bitter and foul thing I had ever tasted. Obviously we had to finish the glass, suppressing involuntary shudders.

"You like?"

"Er... very nice."

"Good. I give you another."

"It's very good of you but we haven't got any small change." He looked hurt.

"I not charge you, my friends. You need it this hot day."

Before we could stop him we had a second dose in our hands and an obligation to swallow it. I nearly vomited. It had a terrible after-taste which lasted for several days.

It was now early evening so we abandoned our plans and took the road to Nicosia and the owner of our motorcycle. All our problems had eaten a large hole in our financial resources and we hoped to receive compensation for the new parts, repairs and labour. He claimed to be sympathetic but said he had no money unless we could find him a new customer for the following week (some hope!). On our next visit to the capital we had another go at the garage proprietor, managing to screw out of him a small sum in no way representative of our costs.

We were very philosophical about all these mechanical difficulties which to some extent had added to our enjoyment and appreciation of Cypriot culture and its most helpful inhabitants. But in our second week a darker cloud loomed over us. It was called Wendy. Gordon had told me that he had a cousin working in Cyprus and that he felt obliged to make a courtesy visit and see how she was getting on. Wendy was a twenty-year-old girl working as a nanny for the wife of a British Army colonel. We duly found the colonel's house in the outskirts of Nicosia and met up with the girl. She was immature and rather silly, looking and acting nearer sixteen than twenty. After we had all walked round town she said that the rest of the day and evening were her own and asked if we would take her over to see Famagusta and have dinner at our hotel. We pondered.

"Only if we can hire, and indeed afford, another motorbike and an extra meal," Gordon said.

"Money's no object; I've got some," she said.

We did find another bike, a Matchless 350, so followed her suggestion. Gordon, who then had to return her to Nicosia, did two round trips that day, a total of 160 miles. On his late return he said, "Her employer has given her tomorrow off to spend time with her cousin! Yes, I know," he added, catching my expression, "I don't want to be lumbered with her either, but I am."

So the next day we both rode into Nicosia, extended the hire on the second machine and took her for a tour, including St Hilarion, Bellapais and Kyrenia where we hired a boat for an hour's sail. Once more Wendy came back for dinner and Gordon did his round trip again. On his return he had further alarming news.

"The colonel's wife invited me in and asked me when my leave expired, which is four more days. She then said that she would give Wendy the rest of that time free to spend with me. When I protested that I couldn't really afford to keep the second bike or pay for meals and other extras, she pressed a good sum of money into my hand to be returned any time in the future if I felt like it!"

In the morning Gordon fetched his cousin again and we gave ourselves a bit of a break by having a lazy day swimming and sunbathing on the beach. Wendy assured us that money would not be a problem; all she had to do, if necessary, was to get an advance on her next month's salary, which she had done before. After the evening meal we strolled out into town and sat having a quiet drink in Krinos, a very smart and respectable café that we had used several times. All over the island we had moved freely about in towns and villages, enjoying food or drinks in cafés or hospitable private houses, with no hindrance. We didn't know, or possibly had forgotten, that in towns such places should only be visited by servicemen if they were displaying an 'In Bounds' sign. Krinos wasn't and two of the omnipresent Army Military Policemen came in, started checking papers officially and taking names and numbers. We managed to slip out before they reached us. I was absolutely furious as it was a very nice place and I felt that international relations were hardly fostered by such aggressive behaviour. But, in retrospect, perhaps the police knew something we didn't...

Next morning we decided that we would have another go at our aborted full tour of the island, but in the reverse order of our previous plan. This enabled us to go via Nicosia where we picked up Wendy. This time we completed the trip, spending some ten hours in the saddles. Approaching our hotel in the evening gloom, mechanical troubles struck again – to both machines. Mine suffered a complete failure of the battery while Gordon had his dynamo pack up. The most illumination we had between us was a glimmer from Gordon's parking light. After dinner he attempted to take Wendy home but after a mile or so at snail's pace he accepted that he would never manage the whole journey in the pitch black night, and came back.

"What shall we do?" he asked Wendy.

"Oh, I expect the hotel can find me a room," she said casually.

"Well, one of us will have to phone and explain to your boss why you are staying out."

She shrugged. "You can if you like but the only phone she's got is the colonel's private wire to Military Headquarters. Urgent messages can be phoned to the Larnaca Road Police Station on the other side of the road. They will deliver a message." So Gordon did that, trying to get the facts across to a policeman with only a basic knowledge of English.

The next day, after spending yet more time and money on our unreliable vehicles, we left Wendy on the beach and both went into Nicosia, as the Matchless bike was due back. As a final protest the battery on the other machine, a new one we had had to purchase, fell off completely. We tied it back on somehow. We went round to the colonel's residence and Gordon went in to reassure the lady of the house. He emerged white and shaking.

"God knows what that policeman told her," he said. "She's fired Wendy. When we bring her back she's going to be put on the first flight out to England without any further pay. I am to return the money she lent me before I leave Cyprus. She has informed the Military Police and the civil police of the debt and if it's not paid I will be arrested and dealt with by her husband!"

"Didn't you try to explain?"

"Of course. You didn't see her in full flood!"

"What do we do now?"

"Don't know. It's not your problem," he added.

"Maybe," I said, "but we'll try and solve it together."

We returned to Famagusta and told Wendy. She shrugged unconcernedly. "Good. I hate that cow and Cyprus stinks anyway!"

We took stock of the financial situation. We had hired a second motorcycle and spent large sums on various repairs and replacements, together with the costs of extra petrol and refreshments. All of this had used up a great deal of money. There was still part of our hotel bill to be settled, the cost of

Wendy's room and meals and, of course, the considerable debt owed to the colonel's charming lady. We opened our wallets and pooled our resources.

"You said you had a sum of money," Gordon said to his cousin. She searched her handbag and produced two pounds.

"Is that it?"

"Yes."

We were in serious trouble. Well, mostly Gordon was in serious trouble. Leaving the island without settling all the debts would lead to all sorts of disasters, even, we wondered, a Court Martial. No young men in those days had a bank account and credit cards hadn't been invented. It was cash or nothing.

"We ought to be able to get something back from the motorcycle man, didn't we?" Gordon speculated desperately. "After all, we've replaced plug, tyres and battery and had various repairs done, all at our expense so far."

"I shouldn't hold out hope for that, based on his previous reaction. Wait until then and get nothing and we're really up the creek," I replied. We sat despondently, watching a new lot of guests booking in, then realisation dawned that we knew two of them; they were boys from RAF Abyad! We engaged them in earnest conversation, explaining our predicament in some detail. With considerable reluctance they finally agreed to lend Gordon enough out of their precious funds to cover his needs, on the strict understanding that they would receive within a matter of days a money order to refund them. Profoundly grateful, we wished them a good holiday. In the evening Gordon set off on his final round trip to take Wendy back to her uncertain future and settled his obligation to her employer, who accepted it with bad grace and dismissed him offensively.

On our final morning we settled our other debts and arranged ourselves on the remaining bike again. Returning the machine in considerably better condition than that in which we had taken it, we argued hard and long for compensation. Eventually he shrugged and said, "You are quite right. I must do something about your expense and trouble." He went into his office and emerged with a voucher for a fortnight's free hire any time in the next year that we wanted. We knew, and no doubt he believed, that we would not be coming back, but that worthless piece of paper was all that we could get out of him. After a final visit to the Ver de Luna to reclaim our peaked caps and say farewell to the friendly and hospitable staff and we were off to the airport after a holiday of mixed emotions but many fond memories.

Back at Abyad Gordon made immediate arrangements to convert money into a form that could be sent to our saviours. His story was treated with some suspicion at the Field Post Office but he managed to get a money order and sent it off. I think he must have wangled an official loan.

A couple of months later I received a personal letter from Wendy, posted in England. It was written in a childish hand and worded in an immature manner. The substance of it was that she was a silly girl and had been reflecting on the trouble she had caused us. She apologised for this and regretted not having thanked us for looking after her for four days. She had wanted to spend so much time with us because she had been so miserable and homesick and was very happy to be back home with her family.

Gordon read the letter and grimaced. "Very pleased, I'm sure! I won't be seeing her again if I can help it!"

9.   RAF Abyad

After about a year under canvas at Abyad, a place for me in one of the barrack rooms became available. These buildings were brick structures with a wide open veranda all round. Inside was the usual arrangement of beds and lockers down each side under large rotating fans and an overhead rail from which to suspend mosquito nets. In the heat of summer some of us would drag our beds out onto the veranda each night for fresher air and rig our nets over them. The trouble with these nets was that however tightly you rolled them up in the mornings, when you unrolled them in the evening and laboriously tucked the bottoms in all round the beds, you often found a mosquito trapped on the inside, keeping itself quiet until you were about to drop off to sleep. One night a rare sand-storm blew up and the outside sleepers awoke to find that the fine sand had penetrated the mesh of the nets. As they rose they could see the outline of their heads picked out on the pillows and they blew their noses for days.

A luxury that we had not enjoyed in the tented area was the use of native bearers. Each hut had a local man available, for a few piastres a week from each inmate, to make the beds, polish shoes, press clothes and generally keep kit up to standard. We became quite friendly with these people, exchanging views in our few words of dodgy Arabic and their attempts at English. I don't think either of us could make head or tail of the others' way of life.

"Hello, raff boy."

"Kweiss, effendi" (Are you well, mate?)

"Oh yes, and you?"

"Kweiss Tamam." (Very well) "Owey, owey, owey" (Very much)

"I do boots?"

"Ayewah". (Yes)

If some disaster befell them, or a friend died, they would say "Marleesh" (Never mind) and "Allah Keefik" (God wills it.)

The brick barracks were provided with a brick built ablutions block. Inside, the facilities for washing and lavatory arrangements were just as basic and unsavoury as those in the tented site.

A consequence of moving accommodation, throughout life in the forces, was the constant acquisition of a whole different lot of friends and acquaintances. One chap in my new surroundings in a four-year engagement had served at a number of home postings and a period in Germany before coming on to Egypt. I asked him how he could have managed all this, including two overseas spells.

"Ah, well, I wasn't in Germany for a full tour. You see, I got a Fraulein up the spout and got posted out here pretty sharpish."

"The Air Force let you abandon your responsibilities?"

He laughed. "Oh, that was their idea, not mine. I was moved for the Air Force's benefit. They don't want to get involved in sorting things out with irate German parents, so in cases when the family come along to track down the culprit they are told that he has been posted away, the destination being classified information."

"So you are a father?"

"I suppose so, but I'll never know!"

Thrown together for so long, our conversation and in particular odd phrases or verbal peculiarities became irritatingly repetitive. One chap was always trying to annoy another, whose surname was Jelly. Upon the latter's appearance the 'comedian' could be guaranteed to call out "Oh look! It must be jelly 'cos jam don't wobble like that," ad nauseam until we took to throwing things at him. Another lad's irritating habit was to call out "Exhibish! Exhibish!" every time someone uncovered his lower half. He was supposed to be mimicking the cries of the barkers outside the sex exhibitions in the disreputable and 'out of bounds' backstreets of larger towns. In these places, it was rumoured, you could watch women performing unspeakable acts with donkeys and many other unlikely activities. However, all these feats were in the same realm as the Indian Rope Trick, inasmuch as you never spoke to anyone who had seen them personally, only someone who had heard it from a chap whose mate had been.

I got friendly with a lad called Eric who was an Instrument Mechanic by trade. He had been allocated an interesting and worthwhile job repairing various important aircraft instruments and refurbishing their dials by repainting the hands and numerals with green luminous paint. The place where he worked was an underground bunker isolated from the rest of us. Being a jeweller in civilian life he would undertake the repair and cleaning of our watches as a side-line and advise us that all you could do with those purchased from the street traders was to throw them away. He was constantly unwell with some mysterious ailment and spent several periods in the military hospital, where I visited him. I often wonder what became of him and whether his problems arose from his proximity to the canisters of radioactive luminous paint.

One way of passing the time was in the creation of elaborate 'demob charts', to be ticked off as the days dragged by. Asked how much time we had left to serve, many of us could reply on the lines of "One year, two months, thirteen days, ten hours, forty-six minutes and twelve seconds." Rubbish, really, because we didn't know what time of day it would be when we actually became free men, or even the exact day.

Sometimes, to provide something to think about, chaps might try to grow moustaches. There was more to this enterprise than might be imagined. The snag was that at all times the photograph on your '1250' had to be an accurate representation of your appearance. Once in possession of a proper moustache you could, in theory, get a new mug-shot done and arrange for an immediate change in your identity card, but at any intermediate stage you could be in trouble. The only hope of achieving success was to combine the attempt with a reasonable period of leave during which time, not being eligible for duties of any sort, you kept a low profile. By omitting to shave a few days before the leave it was hoped that sufficient growth had appeared by the end of it. In practice, the majority who had moustaches were those who started out with them before they joined.

As time passed and the general situation was judged to have relaxed somewhat, it became possible to make excursions further afield. Travelling north up the canal road you came to Deversoir Point, a dot on the map where the Suez Canal emerged into the Great Bitter Lake. It was a great place to view the passing shipping and in a way it was a swimming resort, a diving board having been erected out over the water. There was plenty of beach, of course; it stretched for hundreds of miles. The only building in the immediate area was a small café where we could have a cold drink. It advertised 'hot meals' and one day, after a dip, several of us decided to try the cuisine. We entered and sat at a table. An Arab bustled up and asked what we would like.

"What have you got?"

"You tell me what you want."

"But we don't know what you can do."

"I can do anything you want. Just name it."

It was a modest place with a tiny kitchen.

"Steak?" one of asked tentatively.

"Sure." He wrote it down.

"Fish and chips?" someone else asked, with the same response. And so it went, other requests including chicken, assorted vegetables and puddings, all meeting with a similar reaction. He disappeared into the kitchen and we waited. We waited some more and finally called out. There was no reply so we went into the kitchen. The whole place was entirely deserted and there was no sign of any preparation or cooking. In the end we decided to have another swim.

After an hour or more, our attention was attracted by a distant figure wheeling a pushbike across the sand. Over the handlebars hung a dead chicken and assorted carrier bags. Under the crossbar was slung a sack of potatoes and other vegetables in bags were suspended either side of the rear wheel. He pushed the bike up to the café and went in. Soon the sounds and aromas of cooking could be detected and, well over two hours after placing our orders, we sat down to delicious meals, comprising everything we had ordered.

Further up the canal again, on the shore of Lake Timsah, was Ismailia, which we usually contracted to 'Ish'. This was an important town, a lot of it French in character, developed as part of the Suez Canal complex, and indeed the site of the company's headquarters. A relatively small number of streets were 'in bounds' to British troops, but they were very pleasant with a number of shops and cafés, a smart park kept green by means of perforated pipes buried under the grass supplying constant water, and a number of attractive buildings including a beautiful railway station. It was a good place for buying souvenirs and having a meal. A popular restaurant served massive steaks, done to individual requirements. They were tasty but very hot and I've always suspected that I was eating camel.

Things eased further and eventually we were allowed to travel right up the canal to Port Said, which we invariably pronounced 'Sed'. Well, that's how it's spelled, isn't it? Here, again, in a carefully selected and patrolled section, we could stroll along the harbour road, admire the statue of Ferdinand de Lesseps and watch the men in all the little 'bum' boats trying to sell trinkets to the passengers in the big ships queuing up to take their turn in the slow one-way progress down to Suez, the Great Bitter Lake serving as a passing place. Shops and cafés along the front again provided interesting shopping and intriguing catering.

The long stretch of road north of Ismailia to Port Said ran largely through a barren landscape with the canal almost below ground level and often all that could be seen was an apparently continuous stretch of shimmering sand. The sight of a large ocean-going vessel gliding slowly along, seemingly through an unbroken expanse of desert, was odd.

We didn't make these excursions very often. There wasn't anything new to see or do after a good first visit and little inducement to make the effort in the hottest part of the day to get off a bed, get ready and go.

Occasionally, a couple of us would make the more local trips on a motorbike. There was, on camp, a flourishing motorcycle club. The machines were not members' own, brought out from home, naturally, but a collection of cast-offs of various ages and conditions, which could be borrowed for the afternoon. The dedicated club members had made their hut a cosy meeting room with a home-made bar. Some of them adapted bikes by stripping them down to the bare skeleton, cutting sections of the frame out and re-welding it to shorten the wheelbase. The machines did not get much road use, places to go being limited; rather they were used for trials and scrambles, when this modification improved handling, or so they believed. Outside the perimeter of the camp, a few hundred yards away, the sand rose gradually through foothills towards the highest peak for miles. It was not a great mountain and you could climb easily to the summit, where a large flat rock bore the painted inscription 'JEAN STEPHANOU 1950'. From this viewpoint you could see stretches of the zone in both directions and the expanse of the Great Lake. The terrain on the slopes was a mixture of hard rock, soft sand and shingle and made a good venue for the various motorcycle events and competitions that were staged at intervals, much of the camp turning out to watch.

Seeking something to do, I occasionally played a few rather lethargic games of tennis. The hard courts, like the Motor Transport yard, had been produced by rolling and watering the sand repeatedly until the heat had given it the smoothness and character of hard concrete. I turned my ankle over during one desperate attempt to return an ace and hobbled back to my quarters. There was no way that I was going through all the rigmarole of reporting sick, so I put up with it, limping painfully to work for some time. Several years after my return to 'Civvy Street' I twisted it badly again and reported to the X-Ray department of my local hospital.

"You haven't broken anything this time," they told me.

"What do you mean, *this time*?" I queried.

"You have a healed fracture to a small bone, broken, I should say, three or four years ago."

The camp also had a photographic club and eventually I joined this. The heat of the day made it impossible to be shut in one of the darkrooms until evening, but even then technical problems presented themselves. The first film I developed produced unexpected results. The clubhouse stood well away from any other buildings and the 'cold' water tap was fed from a pipe buried under the sand that absorbed the full heat of the sun. I loaded my film into a lightproof developing tank to be processed by the 'time and temperature' method. The manufacturer of the chemicals provided helpful charts of the development times for various temperatures. Our water was way above these limits so I did some hopeful calculations and shortened the developing time further. Having developed, rinsed, fixed and washed the warm film, I removed it from the tank and held it up to the light. I appeared to have produced a reasonable set of negatives. The final operation prior to hanging the film up to dry, or so I had been taught, was to squeegee excess water off by pulling it through two fingers pressed together. I did that and ended up with a handful of sticky emulsion and a completely clear strip of film. I didn't do that the next time! The warmth of the chemicals also had an effect on printing and it was possible to produce reasonably contrasty prints only by using the hardest grade papers.

Mornings at work continued to drag, enlivened by the sporadic bursts of occasional work and rare moments of excitement. One day someone rushed in and shouted, "It's raining!" It was too, for about the only time in two years, and we all rushed out, stripped to the waist, as we usually were in the hot workshop, and romped about in delight. Another incident to break the monotony was announced by the noisy arrival outside of a police truck and an ambulance. Someone came round from the next-door shop and said "Old Tubby's killed himself!"

Our excitement subsided into sombre concern. Tubby was a recent arrival on the scene, having got married and enjoyed a brief honeymoon immediately prior to his overseas posting. He had volunteered to make the mid-morning tea, saying he knew the fastest way to boil water. Pulling on rubber gloves he had picked up two mains leads and plunged them into the boiler. The gloves must have been faulty. Apparently he went quite blue. In due course the poor young widow was flown out for the funeral and one of my acquaintances was detailed to be part of the guard of honour. He returned from the experience in serious mood. The coffin, albeit draped with a flag, was driven to the military cemetery on the back of a spruced-up coal truck. The guard lined up and let off a joint burst of rifle fire in salute. No-one had warned the unfortunate girl, already in a distressed state, who jumped in the air and dissolved into hysterics.

Reports started to be made of various personal items going missing and these were eventually discovered among the effects of a young Welsh airman, inevitably known as Taffy, who was arrested, charged, court-martialed and sentenced to imprisonment for several months. With an escort of two other airmen he disappeared from the scene. The escorts returned with an account of a grim-looking centre some-where in the distant desert, where everyone, even innocent escorts, were shouted at and had to proceed everywhere at the double. As Taffy's kit was inspected on arrival, a camera, not belonging to him, was discovered. His kleptomania had compelled him to appropriate it even on his way to his punishment. His sentence was summarily doubled. We saw him once more, briefly, many months later, when he re-turned to Abyad before a final discharge. He looked terrible, several stones lighter and with closely cropped hair. Accord-ing to his description of the prison and its regime it must have resembled the establishment in the film 'The Hill' starring Sean Connery.

Looking once more for something to pass the time I joined the church choir. The camp church was another of the attractive purpose-built amenities constructed from the local sandstone. One of the choir members was a charming lady whose husband was the civilian manager of the station's electricity generating plant. This hospitable couple used to invite some of the choir round to their home in the married quarters area for cool drinks and pleasant conversation in the evenings on their veranda among palms and other exotic plants that they had encouraged to grow. These evenings were the most civilised periods that I experienced there.

Throughout the entire period the guard duties continued to come round every ten days or so with monotonous regularity, with the occasional special parade thrown in to remind us to keep drill up to standard. To celebrate the visit of some high-ranking official we were all turned out on the square and formed up on three sides, in the stand-at-ease position, under the full glare of the sun. There was a considerable delay pending the arrival of the VIP who was either late or enjoying the comforts of the Officers' Mess.

Eventually some of us started to sway noticeably; I felt slightly unsteady myself. No-one took any notice and before long one chap fell headlong on the ground. Two others were ordered to grab him under the arms and remove him. He was dragged off, face down, with his nicely polished toecaps scraping along the tarmac all the way, protesting "I'm alright now!" All this could have been prevented if only we had been brought to attention a few times while waiting, which would have been sufficient to liven up our circulation.

It was on the same occasion that one chap, lacking concentration, omitted to ease his rifle forward on the command 'Slope Arms' and thrust his bayonet straight up into his armpit. In due course we marched off, saluting the flag as we passed the flagpole. One morning, as the official ceremony of hoisting the flag was about to be carried out, it was realised that an object had already been pulled to the top. It was one of the oversized toilet buckets, full to the brim with a pungent mixture of urine and disinfectant, obviously the late night prank of one of the revellers from the airmen's bar. With some reluctance someone had to lower it, not without receiving some of the contents on the way down.

Eventually we had to undergo another Free From Infection inspection, conducted in a manner that was even more degrading than usual. Some bright Medical Officer considered that his task would best be performed if we were ordered to strip off all our nether garments and lie back on our beds with our legs spread-eagled over the sides so that the parts to be inspected were displayed most prominently. Among a number of indignities suffered in the course of duty, I think this was the most embarrassing.

After 18 months or so confined to the immediate area of the camps in the Canal Zone and a few carefully restricted parts of towns further up the canal, the situation was deemed relaxed enough to permit a series of coach trips to Cairo to be made. Arrangements must have been agreed with the Egyptian authorities because there were very strict rules applying. Civilian clothing had to be worn, but we were under the orders of an officer and could follow only a predetermined guided tour, under no circumstances moving away from the party, as none of us had a passport. I joined one of these trips and in the early morning climbed into a coach of some vintage that had un-upholstered seats of hard wooden slats.

The journey, one hundred miles on road surfaces that were mostly rough and frequently covered with loose sand blown on from the surrounding desert, took over three hours as our anatomy acquired corrugations. Picking up a local guide we were taken to the Citadel area for a look round, taking in the panoramic view of the large city, and in particular to see the mosque where we had to slip on canvas overshoes before entering. In the magnificent interior we marvelled at the alabaster pillars, several feet thick. The guide lit a magnesium flare and walked round a pillar; you could see the light through it all the way round. He drew our attention to the spectacular pulpit with marble stairs.

"That was a gift from King Farouk before we threw him out", he said, and spat at the mention of the name. From there we were conducted through the lanes and narrow alleys of the perfume market where the local versions of the famous international brands were on sale for a fraction of their price. Then it was over to the Egyptian Museum and, most importantly of all, the stunning artefacts from Tutankhamen's tomb including the truly outstanding golden mask. In the museum the WCs in the men's toilet were a novelty. Alongside the familiar cubicles, equipped with conventional pans with seats, were several modelled on the primitive native arrangements of a hole in the ground on either side of which was an indented footprint, but all moulded in modern tiling.

The coach then took us out to the pyramids and sphinx. We crossed the wide and rather murky Nile and travelled through the outskirts of the city, seeing the inhabitants going about their normal civilised lives in the pleasant surroundings of decent buildings and streets, far removed from the poverty-stricken existence of the poorer classes along parts of the canal. By the Mena House Hotel at Giza the city turned abruptly into desert and we climbed over a hillock to approach the historical site. The Great Pyramid was impressive, rising to a height of 450 feet, but at first sight the sphinx was disappointing. For centuries it had been buried up to the neck in drifting sand but was now excavated all round. As we strolled down towards its backside all that could be seen from a distance was the small head but as we got round the front we could see its magnificence and size, which was only relatively small when viewed from the proximity of the pyramids. It was a pity that the nose was missing, due not to the ravages of 4,500 years of history but to the fact that Napoleon's troops used it as a practice target, it was said.

Time being limited we were given the choice between exploring the narrow passages of the Great Pyramid or queuing up for a camel ride. I chose neither, strolling round to take photographs while others attempted to climb the outside of the pyramid or the outside of a camel. The pyramid's stone blocks were over half the height of a man and although recognised climbing places existed, the climbers didn't get very far. I believe climbing is not now allowed. In no time at all we had to return to the coach for the uncomfortable ride home, having enjoyed a wonderful outing, hoping that the soreness in our posterior regions would not last too long.

For the final few months of my time in Egypt my working life took a turn for the better and, for the first time, I found myself in a proper and necessary occupation after being transferred to the Accumulator Charging Room.

The charging process was undertaken slowly and the section was in operation round the clock, necessitating a shift system of 6am to 2pm, 2pm to 10pm or through the night in rotation. (I should say, of course, 0600, 1400 and 2200 hours). The disadvantage of this arrangement was that although when on night shift you could legitimately spend the days in bed to get some sleep, you got no sympathy from your fellow inmates, who seemed deliberately to make as much noise as possible or perhaps even tip you out of bed as a 'joke'. The advantage was that you could be sure of having two full sheets to sleep between. The arrangement for laundering bed linen was that each week you handed in one of your sheets to the designated orderly who recorded the quantity and took them off to the *dhobi*. When he went to collect and sign for the finished sheets they were stacked high in a neat pile. To check the quantity all he could do was to count the folds. Almost invariably though, someone, no doubt the civilian workers, had stolen some but arranged the remainder in a manner that displayed the correct number of folds. Unless you were in the barracks when they arrived there might not be a sheet left for you. The remedy, the next week, was to tear your sheet in half and send one half off, ensuring that you rushed back from work in time, or as a shift worker were already there, to grab a whole clean one. With a bit of luck you were back to two complete sheets in a week or two.

Separately you also sent off clothes to the dhobi, a building where native workers scrubbed and hammered at your laundry before hanging it out to dry in a large compound. Copious quantities of starch were used, sprinkled on the clothes and sprayed with water before ironing. The workers filled their mouths with water from a bottle and spat it out in a fine spray. When the bush jackets returned you had to force your arms into the sleeves, raising a cloud of starch. Eventually, what with constant laundering, starching and our perspiration, the backs of the light brown jackets turned white.

Work in the charging room was satisfying and rewarding as it was vital to the operation of all the flying in the vicinity. A few of the batteries that came in were standard types used on the Motor Transport Section's vehicles and officers' cars, but the vast majority were the specialised accumulators used in aircraft. All the batteries were booked in and the dates of charge recorded, but those from the airfield were given special treatment, being so important to the efficiency of the electrical systems on an aeroplane. They were charged at constantly monitored rates throughout the slow process and at prescribed intervals were subject to a controlled discharge to measure and record their holding capacity. When through use this fell below the acceptable limit the battery was taken out of active service.

The concentrated sulphuric acid came in large glass carboys packed in straw within a metal cage and as necessary had to be diluted to working strength. This highly dangerous operation had to be carried out under the strictest of regulations, following the instructions on Poster 20. Fully protective clothing, including goggles and thick rubber gloves, had to be worn and quantities of an alkali were kept on hand in case of accidents. Most importantly, you had to know whether carefully to add water to acid or the other way round; the wrong way would produce an explosive boiling, scattering acid in all directions.

For some reason the mess supplied us with unlimited quantities of cocoa in large tins, which we mixed to a consistency that would support a tea spoon unaided and drank in place of tea or coffee, even though it was not the best stimulant for keeping one awake during the long night shift.

We got friendly with a corporal dog-handler. Normally we wouldn't be consorting with the dreaded Station Police but the men of the dog section were a bit more approachable. The corporal would drop into the charging room on his night patrols for a mug of our delicious cocoa and a chat. He always stood just inside the slightly open door with his beautiful German Shepherd outside on the other end of its leash.

"Can't we say 'Hello' to the dog?" we asked.

"No you can't. He's trained to distrust, or even attack, anyone other than me." Sometimes the dog would spot something moving in the dark and the corporal would be jerked violently backwards into the night, spilling cocoa everywhere. As we went on or came off shift at six o'clock in the morning the airmen's mess was open for the likes of us and men on guard duty who fancied an early breakfast. The friendly and obliging duty cooks would serve any food of your choice.

With the approach of my demob-date I found myself talking to an officer who had responsibility for discussing one's future life, either in respect of a career or, he hoped, a further term of service life.

"What do you intend to do with your life?"

"I'm going to look for a job in an electrical company, exploiting my Air Force qualifications."

"Really? You do realise that you won't be accepted by the Trade Union, which is virtually compulsory throughout the industry, unless you have achieved the rank of Junior Technician?" No I didn't; another example of how the whole picture had been kept from us.

"Then may I put in for the exam?"

"Only in due course if you're prepared to sign on for a longer period. You can't get promotion to that rank with less than seven years' service"! I took this in.

"No, four years is enough. I'm going back to Civvy Street."

In May 1955, three months before my discharge, I received a letter, laboriously typed out, there being no photocopiers then, from the Ministry of Labour and National Service in my home town, telling me about the large number of interesting vacancies always available and all the training possibilities. Special concessions were made for ex-servicemen and I was urged to call on them on my release.

Time for excursions was running out but I did get to Ismailia again where I went into a shop that had a recording machine, asked the proprietor to put on some local background music and cut a disc to post off home with a personal message:

"Hello, Mum and Dad. I'm speaking to you all the way from Ismailia in Egypt. I know I've only got about six weeks to go now but I thought this may not only make a personal record for you to hear but also a souvenir for when I come home. As you can hear in the background there is some Egyptian music playing; I got the chap to put some on for you. I don't know whether you will like it. Give my regards to everyone at home. I'm up in 'Ish' for pretty well the last time. I shall probably come up again, have a shop round and take a few last snaps. Best of luck, everybody. Cheerio! Now listen for a bit to the music for the last part of the record."

During the last few weeks of my term of service, the end of which coincided with the expiry of my two years of overseas duty, it was obvious that something was happening on the political front, although we were not told anything.

Mysterious markings were stencilled on all equipment and this, we found, was going on all up and down the canal. It transpired that before long the British presence in the Zone was to be withdrawn and camps and depots taken over by Egypt's own military personnel. The stencilled characters were to distinguish between those items that could be left behind and those that were important enough to send back home. The usual crop of imaginative stories circulated, following the massive full inventory that had to be conducted, such as: there were enough spare aircraft wings up and down the zone to replace those on every 'plane four times over; there were several thousand more left boots than right boots and there were enough WRAF's knickers for every girl to be given several hundred pairs.

"There you, are" said one man, "I told you they don't wear any."

These stories were, naturally, apocryphal, although it certainly was a recognised practice that storekeepers, not bothering to locate items on their shelves somewhere, would regularly just indent for further supplies regardless and, in the event of long delivery dates, just indent once again. By the time I left for home several establishments were already flying the Egyptian flag.

When my turn came, I said goodbye to my mates and went through the farce of returning stores and signing out. With a group of other 'time expired' individuals I was taken down the road to the transit camp to draw bedding and await instructions. On two days running we returned our bedding to stores and were about to climb on a lorry when the plans were changed. It seemed that officers and their families had priority on airplanes without advance booking and our seats were repeatedly reallocated. Eventually we got away and after the long haul back to England landed at an airfield in Wiltshire.

The countryside was incredibly green. It had been raining and the grass by the runway was wet. We jumped up and down in it with glee, some even rolling about on the ground. We transferred to an overnight depot, handed in all our tropical kit but retained our 'blues' and were given a medical examination. They told us that we were to be returned to civilian life in as good a condition as when we left it, even, we were led to believe, being kept back in service until cured if necessary. We were advised not to donate blood for a year as the heat of the desert for two years would have thinned it down. After the examination and an eyesight test we were all declared A1 fit and released.

It was August 7th 1955 and I was a civilian again!

But...

10.   A Civilian Again

We were returning to civilian life but we weren't entirely beyond the reach of the Royal Air Force for some years. For the first eighteen months, as I had always expected, I was transferred to a Reserve Class of service.

The first thing to be done, on the way home, was to report to the depot that issued 'demob suits'. It was explained to us that as an alternative to a suit, casual clothing would be available. The depot was at Woking and we were given railway warrants to get us there and then on to our home destinations. At the Civilian Clothing Depot we were all handed a list of the items to which we were entitled:

> "One single-breasted suit or one sports coat and a pair of flannel trousers, one raincoat, one hat, one shirt with two collars, one tie, one pair of shoes black or brown, two studs, two pairs of socks, one pair of cuff-links and one carton to contain the above."

Even for civilian life the authorities could not envisage anyone wearing a shirt with attached collar! As one man we all asked for the sports coats but were informed that none of it was available. It was a double-breasted suit or nothing and would we please not complain as it was all free. Back home I ventured out in this gear once. The suit was a brown chalk-striped affair with turn-ups and enormous lapels and the hat was a wide-brimmed trilby. I looked like the worst possible type of spiv or gangster and attracted so much derision that I never wore it again, except as fancy dress.

Having collected all this stuff I had to get myself up to and across London and out to my home, at intervals struggling to get the kitbag balanced on my shoulder while holding a large cardboard carton under the other arm. Outside my local railway station a taxi was waiting for customers. I climbed in, still of course wearing uniform. Another airman came out of the station and climbed in beside me and the driver shot off up the hill.

"You haven't asked us where we want to go," I pointed out.

"RAF Bovingdon, don't you?" he asked in surprise.

"He might, but I want to go into town. Still, as I've waited two years for this moment I don't mind a little detour. Take him there first then take me home."

After a short trip out into the country we returned and drove through the main shopping area of Hemel Hempstead. I didn't recognise much of it. A lot of the demolition and new building to transform a sleepy old town into a modern satellite of London had taken place in the two years I had been away. My parents welcomed me home with open arms and my father helped me in with all my gear.

"You must be pleased to be home at last," my mother commented. I replied automatically in the vulgar conversational mode that had become second nature, without a moment's consideration.

"I should think I fucking am!" I said with feeling.

There was now time to study properly the various documents that had been handed to me. I was transferred to Class 'E' of the RAF Reserve, my Reserve Centre being at Kenley in Surrey. I was not to enlist in any other branch of the military or go abroad without permission and must report any change in circumstances such as address, marriage, job, medical state or death! I could, during the next year and a half, be called upon to undertake not more than twelve days consecutive training during each training year. It was my privilege to volunteer for additional training in periods of at least fifteen days. A revised version of the '1250' identity card was issued for retention, to be maintained in pristine condition and not lost. A notice advised me of my financial situation. Pay for fourteen days had been issued with a further fourteen days to come as a regular serviceman together with a ration allowance for 'terminal leave', and an Income Tax leaving certificate had to be completed and sent off. We were sent a small amount of wages during the Class 'E' reserve, airmen receiving the princely sum of £4-11s-4d a quarter.

A list was provided of the items of uniform, etc, to be retained, which were to be kept in serviceable condition:

No.1 Home dress	1 suit
No.2 Home dress	1 suit
Pyjamas	1 pair
Greatcoat	1
Beret	1
Pullover	1
Boots or shoes	1 pair
Gloves BG[1]	1 pair
Shirts BG	2
Collars BG	4
Socks BG	3 pairs
Towels	2
Tie	1
Kitbag	1
Badges, cap	1
Sticks, button	1
Shoes, canvas	1 pair
Braces	1 pair
Brushes, brass	1

All of this was never to be used or worn without specific authorisation.

---

[1] BG = blue/grey

A blue hardback booklet, *The Royal Air Force Certificate of Service*, listed my service career details and stated that my conduct had been 'Very Good', ability in trades, leadership and cooperation had been 'Good' while my bearing was described as 'Smart'.

I never was called back for any reserve training and I can't think why anyone should have been. All camps were bursting at the seams and we surely could not forget in eighteen months how to obey any orders. In any case, all need to experience military life at all would disappear in only a few years' time with the abolition of National Service. Some had to go to a camp, though, and from all accounts did nothing but amble about with few duties and the luxury of being able to look a bit scruffy with civilian-type hair styles, not really under the jurisdiction of the Station Police as were the permanent residents.

Abandoning all ambitions to be an electrical engineer, I answered an advertisement by the largest employer in the district for clerical workers and was taken on immediately, staying with that company for the next twenty-seven years. With my agreement my father had sold my old motorcycle during my absence abroad and we invested in a second-hand car between us. No more than two months after my return I took a driving test and, to my chagrin, failed the eyesight examination and had to get fixed up with spectacles for short-sightedness. So much for the Air Force's A1 result in the recent past! I don't suppose all that squinting in the sun without the use of standard-issue sunglasses did our eyes any good.

The year after I came home from Egypt, Colonel Nasser 'nationalised' the Suez Canal Company and, as a consequence, before the end of 1956 the Suez Crisis erupted, in which Britain, France and Israel attacked Egypt, with disastrous results, and the canal lost its international status and became fully Egyptian. In the fruitless fighting and disorder, the statue of Ferdinand de Lesseps, architect of the great waterway, was pulled down and thrown into Port Said harbour.

At the end of eighteen months as a reservist, as contracted in my original Attestation, I was, to my surprise, still not released from all obligation. Further correspondence advised that, effective from 6th February 1957, I was discharged from 'Class E' Reserve and transferred to 'Class G' (General) Reserve until either 30th June 1959 or the age of 45, whichever occurred first. The principal provisions of this class of reserve service were that I might be subject to a recall to arms in any emergency and the need for the further notification of any changes in personal circumstances. In the unlikely event of a recall, you were expected to attend with your uniform in good condition, which could have been a bit awkward as towards the end of my standard eighteen months' reserve I had started using it for gardening and other rough jobs! We were asked not to take our medals with us unless we just could not arrange safe custody (ha!). I had to send back at once my '1250' identity card in return for which I received a form 'To Whom It May Concern' stating why I hadn't got one! There were no more wages. I never heard from them again and in June 1959 I finally severed all my connections with the Royal Air Force.

It might be thought that several years under service conditions doing little of importance was a complete waste of time, but most men who entered National Service or short-term contracts will tell you, and it's true, that they were later glad to have done so. All experiences enrich one's existence. Despite the frustrations of inactivity and dictatorial discipline with little or no redress for injustices it was no bad thing to discover that you could exist and look after yourself in all respects of dress and hygiene completely unreliant

upon the services of a good mother or wife, so Nation‹
Service had some redeeming aspects. I've never regretteᴅ
having to go through this experience, although I was disappointed at not having had the award that was made available
for the Coronation. I would have liked to have received a
medal.

However, half a century went by all too quickly and then
something very unexpected occurred. In October 2003 a
friend drew my attention to a newspaper article which
detailed how veterans of the British presence in the Suez
Canal Zone in the 1950s had been pressing ever since for a
campaign medal. I learned a bit more about the military and
political situation of those far-off days. The British garri-
soned troops, who had occupied Egypt since 1882, were put
on alert in October 1951 after the Egyptian Government
abrogated a 1936 Anglo-Egyptian treaty that authorised the
stationing of troops to ensure the free flow of international
shipping in the canal. From that moment, the British faced
attacks from the Bulak Nizam organisation, an auxiliary
Egyptian police force that had official backing to terrorise
the British garrison. Over 50 British servicemen were killed
in action and more died from the general conditions, accidents and disease, with many Egyptian fatalities as well, the
most ferocious battle taking place on January 25th 1952 in
Ismailia. Fortunately I wasn't in the right (or wrong) place or
time to be involved in such fierce activity and was demobi-
lised before the disastrous events of the Suez Crisis in 1956.

Apparently enquiries had been made about the possibility
of a medal in the 1950s, resulting in a decision by the Army
Council that there was no case for one. Recently it became
known that the matter had never been debated at the proper
levels and Tony Blair's government, recognising the injustice,
required it to be considered by a specially formed sub-
committee. In due course the provision of the General